The Mongo Mango Cookbook

And Everything You Ever Wanted to Know About Mangoes

C Y N T H I A   T H U M A

PINEAPPLE PRESS, INC.
Sarasota, Florida

121951

Inquiries should be addressed to:

Pineapple Press, Inc.
P.O. Box 3889
Sarasota, Florida 34230

www.pineapplepress.com

Library of Congress Cataloging-in-Publication Data

Thuma, Cynthia.
The Mongo mango cookbook / Cynthia Thuma.— 1st ed.
p.   cm.
Includes bibliographical references and index.
ISBN 1-56164-239-8 (pbk. : alk. paper)
1. Cookery (Mangoes) 2. Mango. I. Title.

TX813.M35 T48 2001
641.6′444—dc21

2001023489

First Edition
10 9 8 7 6 5 4 3 2 1

Design by Carol Tornatore Creative Design
Printed in the United States of America

Table of Contents

ACKNOWLEDGMENTS vii

FOREWORD xi

I

All About Mangoes 1

Mango Trends 3

Mangoes Everywhere 5

Mango Beginnings 8

Technical Specifications 13

The Mango Family Tree 15

Mango Nuptials 18

II

Using Mangoes 21

The Many and Varied Uses 23

Slicing Mangoes 26

Storing and Freezing Mangoes 28

Using Green Mangoes 30

III

Mango Recipes 31

SCENE SETTERS: APPETIZERS AND SALADS 33

Coconut Shrimp with Mango-Lemon Dip 34

Grand Avenue Mango Salad 35

Las Olas Seafood Salad 36

Mango-Prosciutto Rollups 37

Pineapple-Mango Slaw 38

Troppo Fruit Salad 39

Summer Seafood Salad with Sesame-Mango
Champagne Dressing 40

Yaam 42

MAIN EVENTS: MANGO ENTREES 43

Chicken Stir-fry with Mangoes and Asian Corn 44

Grilled Chicken with Pineapple-Mango Salsa 45

Grilled Pork Chops with Mangoes 46

Islander Chicken 47

Last Key Shrimp Kabobs 48

ON THE SIDE: ACCOMPANIMENTS 49

Bes' Kine Mango Salsa 50

Mangoes Mexicana with Pico Seco 51

Mexican Mango-Jicama Salsa 52

THE FINAL TOUCH: DESSERTS 55

Sticky Rice with Mangoes 56

Mango Mousse 57

Spiced Stewed Mangoes 58

Summer Fruit Salsa 59

Mango-Pineapple Drop Cookies 60

Upside-Down-Under Cake 62

Wikiwiki Fresh Fruit Dessert 63

GET JUICED: NONALCOHOLIC DRINKS 65

B Sting 66

Mango Milkshake 66

Mango Milkshake with Cream of Coconut 67

Gardener's Punch 68

Mango Juice 69

Mango-Orange Frost 70

Miss Mattie's Front Porch Cooler 71

Traditional Lassi 72

Tropical Lassi 72

Whitecap Tropical Freeze 73

BOTTOMS UP: ALCOHOLIC DRINKS 75

Mango Colada 76

Frozen Mango Daiquiri 76

Frozen Mango Margarita 77

Mangria 77

A Trio of Mango Shooters 78

Mariposa 80

COOL CONFECTIONS: ICY TREATS 81

Athlete's Punch Pops 82

Cherry-Mangoberry Frozen Fruit Pops 82

Mango-Coconut Ice Lollies 83

Kulfi and Kulfi Kones for Kids 84

Mango Granita 86

Thai Ice Pops 87

LAGNIAPPE: MANGO MISCELLANY 89

Mango Leather 90

Mango-Nut Bread 91

Robbie's Spicy Ham Glaze 92

Mango–Poppy Seed Vinaigrette Dressing 93

Tropical Trail Mix 94

Ono Ono Tropical Bagel Spread 95

CYBERMANGO: RECIPES ONLINE 97

APPENDIX 1:
Mango-growing Countries 99

APPENDIX 2:
International Mango Cultivars 109

APPENDIX 3:
Nurseries, Garden Clubs, and Festivals 123

SELECTED BIBLIOGRAPHY 131

INDEX 135

Acknowledgments

This book was a labor of love that took more than a decade to create but never would have been possible without the assistance, encouragement, and contributions of many people around the globe and, indeed, throughout cyberspace:

❧ The helpful staffs of the Hawaii Cooperative Extension Service at the College of Tropical Agriculture and Human Resources, University of Hawaii at Manoa; the University of Florida Institute of Food and Agricultural Science, Gainesville; and the Broward County Cooperative Extension Service, Davie, Florida

From academia and governmental agencies:

❧ Rashid Al-Yahyai, assistant lecturer, Sultan Qaboos University, College of Agriculture, Muscat, Sultanate of Oman
❧ Krishnan Bheenick, lecturer in agricultural systems, University of Mauritius, Reduit, Mauritius
❧ Helen Bogdan, public affairs consultant, Republic of Nauru
❧ Dr. Richard Brettell, subprogram leader, Division of Plant Industry, CSIRO Tropical Ecosystems Research Centre, Winnellie, Northern Territories, Australia
❧ Josephine Brown, Agriculture Western Australia, Perth
❧ Dr. Richard Campbell, curator of tropical fruits, Fairchild Tropical Gardens, and professor, Florida International University, Miami
❧ Dr. A. R. Desai, horticultural scientist, Indian Council for Agricultural Research, ICAR Research Complex for Goa, Ela, Old Goa, India
❧ Kelly Elcock, Information Centre, Caribbean Agricultural Research and Development Institute, University of the West Indies, St. Augustine Branch, Trinidad
❧ Juneann Garnett, National Agricultural Research Institute, Research and Documentation Centre, Demerara, Guyana
❧ Hlanganani Gilika, Land Utilisation Division, Ministry of Agriculture, Gaborone, Botswana
❧ Dr. Hernani G. Golez, Agricultural Chief III, Republic of Philippines Bureau of Plant Industry, National Mango Research and Development Center, San Miguel, Jordan, Guimaras, Philippines

- Dr. Costas Gregoriou, tropical and subtropical horticulturist, Agricultural Research Institute, Nicosia, Cyprus
- Dr. Lance Hill, department head and professor of biological science, and Mary Genevieve Ali Balagaize, librarian, University of Papua New Guinea, Port Moresby
- Rowland J. Holmes, extension horticulturist, Queensland Horticulture Institute, Ayr, Queensland, Australia
- Rudy Juan, crops lecturer, and Alfred F. Serano, communication lecturer and acting principal, Belize College of Agriculture, Central Farm, Cayo District, Belize
- Irene Kernot, senior information extension officer, Queensland Horticulture Institute, Mareeba, Queensland, Australia
- Kuo-Tan Li, graduate research assistant, Department of Horticultural Sciences, New York State Agricultural Experiment Station, Cornell University, Geneva, New York
- Dr. Tzong-Shyan Lin, professor of horticulture, National Taiwan University, Taipei
- Jose Loustau-Lalanne, director, Plant Genetic Resources Development Section, Ministry of Agricultural and Marine Resources, Victoria, Mahe, Republic of Seychelles
- Abdallah Maghdad, chief, division of horticulture, Morocco Ministry of Agriculture, Rural Development and Maritime Fisheries, Rabat
- Nancy McGuire, press secretary for Prime Minister Dr. Keith Mitchell, and James Mahon, agricultural assistant, communications unit, Ministry of Agriculture, Lands, Forestry and Fisheries, St. George's, Grenada
- Dr. Mahmoud Medany, director, Agromet Applications Department, Central Laboratory for Agricultural Climate, Giza, Egypt
- Patchara Punjasamarnwong, Technology Transfer Subdivision, Horticulture Research Institute, Department of Agriculture, Chatuchak, Bangkok, Thailand
- Dr. Mark Rieger, professor of horticulture, University of Georgia, Athens
- Manrico Scarpelli, Tirrenia, Italy; Rosalba Risaliti, faculty of agriculture, University of Pisa; and Professors Conticini and Fiorino, faculty of agriculture, University of Florence, Italy
- Seewonlall Seeruttun, research and development officer, Division of Horticulture, Commonwealth of Mauritius Ministry of Agriculture, Food Technology and Natural Resources, Port Louis, Mauritius. Ever patient, gracious, and helpful, Seewon was the "go-to guy" on all issues pertaining to the Indian Ocean rim
- Dr. R. R. Sharma, International Mango Registrar, Division of Fruits and

Horticultural Technology, Indian Agricultural Research Institute, New Delhi, India

❧ Dr. Michael B. Thomas, Centre for International Ethnomedical Education and Research, Gainesville, Florida

❧ Dr. Eli Tomer, chief mango research scientist, Volcani Center of Agriculture Research, Negev, Israel

❧ Steve Wilson, associate lecturer and junior research fellow, Department of Agricultural Science, University of Tasmania, Hobart

From agriculture:

❧ Ali from the South African Mango Growers' Association, Tanzeen

❧ Howard Marguleas, co-founder, Sun World International, Inc., Coachella Valley, California

❧ Bill Pfeil, proprietor, Bill's Farm, Kaunakakai, Molokai, Hawaii

❧ Reny Platz, agricultural manager, Maui Tropical Plantation, Wailuku, Maui, Hawaii

❧ Yvette Ramos, marketing coordinator, Brooks Tropicals, Homestead, Florida

❧ Jeremiah S. Shelembe, Swaziland Fruit Canners Pty., Ltd., Malkerns, Swaziland

❧ Erica Stensgaard Thompson, Sun World International, Inc., Coachella, California

From media and the humanities:

❧ Ron Barrineau, executive director, Northern Marianas Islands Council for the Humanities, Saipan, Northern Mariana Islands

❧ Jean-Luc David, editor, *Te Fenua Fo'ou*, Uvea, Wallis and Futuna Islands

❧ Betsy Raymond Hodde, Delray Beach, Florida, former food and lifestyle editor, *The Hollywood Sun*

❧ Kathy Martin, food editor, *The Miami Herald*, Miami

❧ Marcia Woods, science writer, USDA Agricultural Research Service, Albany, California

From information services:

❧ The cooperative and helpful staffs of the Broward County Library, downtown branch, Ft. Lauderdale, Florida; BCC/FAU College/University Library, Davie, Florida; Palm Beach County Library, southwest county branch, Boca Raton, Florida; the Boca Raton, Delray Beach, Boynton Beach, and Wilton Manors (Florida) city libraries and the Benicia City Library, Benicia, California

🌺 Eppie D. Edwards, deputy director, and the staff of the National Library of Jamaica, Kingston

🌺 Neal Hatayama and Joan Hori, reference librarians, Hawaii State Library, Honolulu

🌺 Susan Mercer, information request services librarian, State Library of New South Wales, Sydney, Australia

🌺 Wendy Morrow, reference librarian, Information Services Department, National Library of Australia, Canberra

🌺 Alan Ventress, Mitchell librarian, State Library of New South Wales, Sydney, Australia

And others:

🌺 Kris Rowland of Pineapple Press, who exercised considerable tact, graciousness, and judiciousness as she helped hone this manuscript into its final form. Good editors are a blessing, and Kris is among the best.

🌺 Dietitian and nutritionist Christie Caggiani, Boca Raton, Florida.

🌺 A very special tip of the hat to some good friends, old and new, who provided essential information, asked pertinent questions, and provided lots of inspiration: Diane Tomasik, Springfield, Virginia; Ann Romer, Richmond, Virginia; Lynnea Ladouceur, New Haven, Connecticut; Carrie Swaby, Kailua, Oahu, Hawaii; Yadi Yu, Boca Raton, Florida; Monica Salazar, Coral Springs, Florida; Tracy Porter, Plantation, Florida; Phyllis Cambria, Coconut Creek, Florida, Barbara Pippin, Ft. Lauderdale, Florida; Mariam Khandwalla, Wilton Manors, Florida; Edgar Duarte, Miami, Florida; and David Reid and Bill Monroe, both of Merritt Island, Florida

🌺 A small army of kind folks provided helpful leads or pieces to the puzzle: Ida Talagi-Hekesi, Niue Information Centre, Alofi, Niue; I. Kivia, Papua New Guinea; Leon Salt, Pitcairn Island; Samir Tanatwi, Giza, Egypt; Dale Hornsby, Baton Rouge, Louisiana; Gorgonio Linterna, Guimaras, Philippines; Margaret Christian, Norfolk Island; and Georgette Woo, Honolulu

🌺 The staff of Fairchild Tropical Gardens in Miami for their Mango Mornings, and the International Mango Festival, which kept me tasting, dreaming, and experimenting.

🌺 My husband, Jim Young, and our son, Nicholas, for their relentless support and good humor, and for little Nick's love of mangoes, which makes me ever so happy

🌺 My parents, Anthony and Madgeline Thuma, and my brother, Joe, whose fondness for mangoes rivaled—and sometimes dwarfed—my own

🌺 And finally, to three hungry Rottweilers named Doogie, Rose, and Tramp, who wolfed down the leftovers with gusto

Foreword

I t simply had to happen. There was no way around it. Benjamin Franklin Hart, the usually gentle but sometimes curmudgeonly obstetrician who helped ease my passage into the world, had been smitten by mangoes. He loved them so much, he wanted to grow them commercially. Unfortunately, the good doctor lived about twenty years before his time. Still, he became south Florida's mango equivalent of Johnny Appleseed, planting mango trees throughout northeastern Broward County, especially in Ft. Lauderdale's Floranada section and in the cities of Oakland Park and Wilton Manors, the town where I grew up.

My dad, who lived in a small apartment atop a tropical nursery in Hialeah when he moved to south Florida, was bitten by the mango bug too. There he was, a nice boy from Long Island, living large and loving it among the mangoes, monstera, canistel, guavas, coconuts, Key limes, and all the rest. I'm sure he thought the garden of earthly delights he lived atop was heaven on earth. One day, my dad met the woman who would later become my mom. She just happened to be one of the nurses who worked for Dr. Hart. You can guess the rest, I'm sure. Their first child simply had to be a mango maniac, and I am—it was in the stars.

My grandparents' home was next to ours. That meant we could grow twice the number of mango trees. We had Tommy Atkins (that we bought from the Atkins family in Ft. Lauderdale) and Haden trees out front, a Keitt between the houses, and a Zill (that we bought from Lawrence Zill himself), a Brooks, and another Haden out back. We also had a neighbor's turpentine tree that shared its bounty with us. Hurricane Cleo took care of the Brooks tree. I never minded because I didn't like its pale, jejune fruit anyway. (I didn't know then about the beauty of green mangoes.) The Keitt, in which my brother's tree house had been constructed, the Atkins, and the Haden in the front yard had to go because they got so big that anytime a fruit dropped on the roof at night, it sounded almost as if a burglar had crashed in through a window. We also worried that someday another hurricane would blow through the area and deposit most of the mango trees in our living room. That hurricane was Andrew, and fortunately, by the time he came calling, those three trees were gone. We're now down to two trees, the Zill and the backyard Haden, plus we're still getting our neighbor's windfall turpentines. The trees are still prolific, and I'm still as smitten by them as when I was a little kid. Now I'm a mom, and my son, Nicholas, although he's only three, shows major promise as a mango maniac himself. That's my boy. Perhaps one day he'll march in the King Mango Strut down in Coconut Grove.

I started writing about mangoes back when I worked for *The Sun-Tattler* in Hollywood, Florida. I created a lot of those recipes, used others from cookbooks that were sent to us by publishers, and even slipped a few of my dad's best recipes in. The recipes in this book are ones created by me, my dad, my brother, Joe, my maternal grand-mom, and my mother, who's quite a mango buff too. She prefers to eat hers plain. She's a purist, you know?

But remember this: it's not apples, bananas, or oranges that are the world's favorite fruit. It's mangoes. Trust me. I know these things. I've spent years doing the research. And I've been groomed to write this book since birth.

I

All About Mangoes

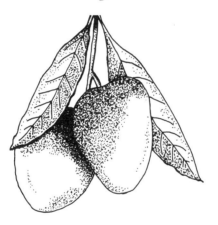

Fruit of the Gods

MANGOES ARE IN

Mango Trends

No argument about it—the mango, sometimes called "king of fruits," is the world's most popular fruit, cultivated in more than one hundred countries. Tennis legend Martina Navratilova won't start her day without one. A city in Florida is named after the mango, and one Florida death-row inmate insisted on one as part of his final meal. Legendary Urdu poet and writer Mirza Asadullah Khan Ghalib pined for mangoes from Calcutta. Marjorie Kinnan Rawlings, author of *Cross Creek* and *The Yearling*, adored them. Henry Ford named his winter estate after them. Suddenly, from sidewalk kiosks in dusty Third World villages to chi-chi beach resorts in Maui, Palm Beach bistros, Sausalito trattorias, Cannes cafes, and tony, trendy restaurants the world over, it's hip to be mango.

Once, fashion's movers and shakers called the warm, vibrant, yellow-orange hue apricot, cantaloupe, or even pumpkin. Now the name of the *tres haute* hue is mango. And if you've got your sniffer attuned to the latest scents, you'll quickly learn mango's fresh, fruity fragrance is a rave in skin and hair care products. Mango lovers probably saw the boom coming with Jimmy Buffet's album *Last Mango in Paris* in the late 1980s. Or perhaps you're a fan of Italian rocker Mango, have heard Oba's album *Wild Mango,* or play Mango Cats on your Palm Pilot.

Formerly thought of by many as a mere Third World fruit, the mango now is in the front line of fashion, in the arts, and on the menu in the world's fanciest restaurants. The glitterati in south Florida cuisine are the cutting-edge chefs known collectively as the Mango Gang: Norman Van Aken, Allen Susser, Mark Militello, Robbin Haas, and Douglas Rodriguez.

How pervasive has the ubiquitous mango become? Check your local bookstore. Some recent titles include *Mango Days: A Teenager Facing Eternity Reflects on the Beauty of Life* by Patty Smith, a poignant memoir by a Punahou School student from Hawaii who waged a valiant but ultimately futile battle against cancer. Also in nonfiction you'll find *Mango Elephants in the Sun* by Susana Herrera, a memoir of her two years in northern Cameroon as a Peace Corps volunteer. Also check out *Spies, Black Ties & Mango Pies: Stories and Recipes from CIA Families All Over the World* by Jean M. Luther and others. Over in the fiction section, there's *The Mango Opera* by Tom Corcoran, *Man or Mango: A Lament* by Lucy Ellman, *Seventeen Ways to Eat a Mango* by Joshua Kadison, and *Murder Under the Mangoes*, a collaborative effort by the CrimeWriters of Queensland, Australia. Dale Hornsby's romantic adventure *Under the Mango Tree* takes place on the island of Boca Del Toro off Panama. Key to the story is the mango, which holds a symbolic meaning for the hero and heroine. Among inspirational books, there's *Eat Mangoes Nude* by Sark. There's even mango-centric kiddie lit, with the classic *House on Mango Street* by Sandra Cisneros, *Green Mango Magic* by Sylvie Hossack, and *Mango Lady and Other Stories from Hawaii* by Ted Gugelyk.

Mangoes Everywhere

*S*ymbols of life and eternal bliss, mangoes have a rich and varied history on their side. A few infobits:

- In India, mangoes are *aam*. In Malaysia and the Philippines, they are called *mangga* or *mempelam*. In Thailand, they are *mamuang mun,* and in Bali, *manggu* or *poh*. They are *qua soai* in Vietnamese, *amra* in Sanskrit, *srai* in Khmer, and *mwembe* in Swahili. In ancient Persia, they were *Samarbehist*—fruit from heaven.
- Buddha, who stayed with his monks in mango groves in Amrapali, Anupiya, Chunda, Mahachunda, Jivaka, Pavarika, and elsewhere, was presented a grove of mango trees by his followers to rest and meditate in. His followers helped introduce mangoes throughout Southeast Asia and began the mango's global odyssey.
- What is now the island nation of Sri Lanka was converted to Buddhism after an earnest discussion about mango trees between Prince Mahinda and King Tissa of Anuradhapura. When the king was convinced of the prince's knowledge and sincerity during their highly symbolic conversation, he converted, which effected the conversion of the remainder of the island's inhabitants.
- In the fourteenth century, the Amir of Khusran called mangoes "the pride of the garden, the choicest fruit of Hindustan."
- The sixteenth-century Mogul emperor Akbar the Great of Hindustan (1556–1605) planted more than one hundred thousand trees at his palace, Laghbakh. The area surrounding his city of Amroha in Darbhanga boasted more than two hundred varieties of mangoes.

❦ Mangoes are mentioned in the *Upanishads*, the Vedic tracts that discuss man's relationship with his universe. They also are mentioned in the *Vedas*, the four sacred books of Hinduism, and are prominent in the *Ramayana*, the third-century epic tale of the travels and conquests of Prince Rama.

❦ Sanskrit poets were especially enamored of both the taste and symbolism of the mango and used mangoes as a frequent metaphor in their writings.

❦ Some mango trees are grown in China's extreme south, in Hainan, Yunnan, and Gungod sheng (provinces). Mao Tse-Tung, who tried them in 1968, was smitten. He called them a "spiritual time bomb." As word of his delight for them spread, Pakistan, which was attempting to gain favor with China, presented Chairman Mao with mangoes and tree saplings.

❦ India's prime ministers have long known that mangoes help make it easy to make high-profile friends. Jawaharal Nehru presented baskets of the fruit to George Bernard Shaw and Soviet leaders Nikita Kruschev and Nicolai Bulganin. Lal Bahadur Shastri wowed Alexi Kosygin with them. Indira Ghandi presented baskets of the highly sought-after Alphonso variety while visiting abroad. Among the luminaries to whom she presented them were American President Jimmy Carter, Soviet Premier Leonid Brezhnev, and Yugoslavian President Marshall Tito.

Mangoes have friends at all strata of society around the globe. Say, for a moment, you're visiting Dussheri Village in Kakori, India, strolling in the shade of the town's famed 250-year-old tree, thought by some to be the oldest living tree. Or you're in Cebu City, Philippines, promenading along Pelaez Street in the shadow of the University of San Carlos. Lining the sidewalks are ramshackle stands groaning with luscious, intoxicatingly aromatic mangoes. Their sweet scent tantalizes you there at ground zero of mangodom.

Mangoes' reputation has exceeded the boundaries of the countries where they are grown. They have long been revered by Europeans as the most luscious of fruits. Pay a few *hryvna* and you can buy a bottle of mango nectar or soda from sidewalk vendors in

Simferopol, the capital city of the Autonomous Republic of Crimea in Ukraine. Or stroll into the giant Julius Meinl supermarket at the end of the chi-chi Graben shopping district in downtown Vienna, and you can purchase mango drinks, yogurt, baby food, and the real thing, imported from Costa Rica and elsewhere. Among Western Europeans, the Swiss are especially smitten with the taste of mango flesh. Stroll the Bahnhofstrasse in downtown Zurich and you'll see all kinds of mango products—drinks, baby food, fruit leather, and the real deal. And all at astronomical prices.

The English word for this noble fruit comes from the word *man-kay*, coined by the Tamil people of southern India, but the name hardly does it justice. Still, in the last decade or so, the mango has expanded its popularity, moving from its Third World background to its rightful place as the world's most popular fruit, with a versatile, exotic taste that holds its own in a variety of recipes. Mangoes also work and play well with other fruits, and they serve as an exotic stand-in for recipes that call for peaches or pineapple too.

From sea to shining sea in Europe, Asia, the United States, and elsewhere, supermarket shelves, gourmet grocers, and greengrocers' bins are groaning with mangoes in their various incarnations. In the U.S., for example, mangoes are available in abundance at Star Markets; at Daiei and hundreds of mom-and-pop groceries throughout Hawaii; at Publix, Winn-Dixie, and Sedano's supermarkets in Florida; and at the giant HEB supermarkets in Texas and California. In other seemingly less likely spots around the country, such as the Shady Maple Market in Lancaster County, Pennsylvania, where Amish families shop, mangoes are popular. And you won't find them in just the produce section. They're also available canned, frozen, dried, and in juices and other beverages and beverage mixes.

Mango Beginnings

The mango is believed to have been discovered as long ago as five to six thousand years in eastern India, Thailand, Myanmar (formerly known as Burma), the Andaman Islands, or Malaysia. When and where the first plant pushed its way up from the rich soil is anybody's guess. Before man ever started tinkering with grafts, it's likely Mother Nature provided a little interspecific hybridization between *Mangifera indica* and *Mangifera sylvatica* and perhaps a few others in the genus *Mangifera*. Hiuen T'sang, a traveler from China, visited Hindustan between A.D. 632 and 635 and became the first foreigner to fall under the mango's spell.

The evergreen trees flourished throughout Asia. India, Indonesia, and the Philippines became major mango-exporting nations. The first group to spill the beans and initiate trade of the fruit were peripatetic Buddhist monks four or five centuries B.C. One theory holds that mangoes first reached Africa by way of Persia in the tenth century. Other theorists contend they reached Africa's shores in northern Somalia by 1331, but despite their earlier introduction, they were not formally and widely introduced until the Portuguese brought them at the dawn of the seventeenth century.

The Portuguese, who successfully experimented with grafting techniques, helped account for the wide variety of mangoes in India as well as their proliferation in appropriately temperate climates throughout the world. Traders from Portugal introduced mangoes to Brazil in the 1700s and to Barbados in 1742; from there, the boom began. Mangoes began popping up all over the world. They arrived in Puerto Rico by about 1750, Jamaica in 1782, Egypt in 1825, and Tahiti in 1848. They even reached the Azores by 1865. Their popularity spread throughout the New World, including the West Indies and Caribbean, the Bahamas, Mexico, southern California, Central America, and parts of South America. Today mangoes are grown as far away as Pakistan, Kenya, and Australia. And they're still spreading. They were introduced in Cyprus in 1982, and in the U.S., amateur horticulturists are experimenting with them in Louisiana. India still reigns supreme, of course: its exports provide about sixty-five percent of the world's supply. But dozens of other nations have gotten in on the act too. In 1985, Spain joined the fun as a mango-exporting nation; Oman jumped in the fray in 1990. Smaller nations such as Guinea, Mauritius, and Reunion are beginning to horn in on the action.

Within the United States, mangoes are grown in five places: throughout Hawaii, in southern Florida, in southern California, in the Rio Grande Valley area in Texas, and in Arizona. Growing mangoes in Arizona requires a greater amount of effort since that state is dry throughout the year, although recently a small cadre of backyard growers have found success. Mangoes thrive in lowland areas, in climates that have dry winters and wet summers. The host climate needs to be warm nine to twelve months a year.

Hawaii: Mangoes were introduced to the Hawaiian Islands in 1824 by Capt. John Meek, although some contend that they were brought there earlier in the nineteenth century by Don Francisco de Paula Marin. Whether or not Marin was the first, he certainly was Johnny Mangoseed there, planting trees on Oahu.

Mangoes remain a popular backyard fruit on all the islands, but because of an infinitesimal weevil, *Cryptorhynchus mangiferae*, that sometimes inhabits the seeds of Hawaiian mangoes, they are not exported in their natural state to the U.S. mainland. The fruit is grown commercially for use on the islands. A variety of treatments and irradiation protocols are in development to allow the mango to be exported widely soon.

Backyard trees on Maui and the Big Island, especially, are laden with fruit during the summer months. Mangoes are popular on menus throughout the Hawaiian Islands, from the most exclusive restaurants to shave-ice stands. Although the fresh fruit is not exported from Hawaii, a variety of delightful jams, jellies, sauces, and chutneys are exported and are worth seeking out.

Southeast Florida: Mangoes were introduced to southeastern Florida in 1833 by Dr. Henry Perrine, but after Perrine's death during the massacre at Indian Key on August 7, 1838, the trees were not properly cared for and died. They were re-introduced by a Dr. Fletcher in 1861, who planted seeds from Cuba. Today on the eastern coast of the state, they are grown as far north as Merritt Island in Brevard County, near the Kennedy Space Center.

In the 1940s and '50s, a curmudgeonly but enterprising Ft. Lauderdale obstetrician/gynecologist, Benjamin Franklin Hart, planted dozens of trees in the northeastern part of the city and the adjoining community of Oakland Park as he toyed with the idea of raising Florida mangoes commercially. He found they could not be transported to markets quickly enough to make them a viable seller. Hart, who left his traditional practice for one in alternative medicine later in his career, was ahead of his time in his mango enterprise too. In the years since then, transportation and handling methods have improved and mango pests have been reduced, allowing devotees all over the world the opportunity to enjoy the favorite fruit of the gods. Fortunately for Broward County dwellers, many of Dr. Hart's mango trees still remain.

Southwest Florida: Mangoes were introduced on Florida's west coast by W. P. Neeld in 1877. The first grafted varieties were introduced by Reverend D. G. Watt in 1885. Since their introduction to Florida, they have grown to become an important cash crop as well as an exceptionally popular backyard tree. South Florida's multicultural population includes many who have migrated from mango-loving countries, so the fruit is highly sought after in the Sunshine State.

Ponce de León called the area he discovered "Land of Flowers," and Floridians are justifiably proud of the beautiful varieties that grow here. They're equally proud of the exotic fruits and vegetables that flourish, especially citrus fruits and mangoes. To wit, the orange blossom is the state flower, and there's a Citrus County. There's also a city (near Seffner in Hillsborough County) named Mango (population

8,700). In Palm Beach County alone, there are twelve streets with the word "Mango" in their names and a city named Mangonia Park. When Miamians wanted to begin an alternative parade to the King Orange Jamboree, they named it the King Mango Strut. The TV cameras roll as the big bands and floats promenade along Biscayne Boulevard for the King Orange Jamboree parade on New Year's Eve, but the real fun is at the Strut in Coconut Grove, along with the Marching Freds and the Precision Briefcase Drill Team.

California: Mangoes came to California in 1880 at Santa Barbara, roughly the same time the first commercial trees were being planted in Australia. In 1993, Sun World International of Coachella Valley, purveyors of exotic fruits and vegetables, began selling Keitt mangoes grown there. The desert conditions cause the sugars within the fruit to become concentrated, making the fruit superb, local growers contend.

Texas and Arizona: Most of the mangoes in these states are grown by exotic fruit fanciers and are not for commercial sale.

Mangoes are proliferating elsewhere in the world, and with ongoing support of growers and extensive research, mangoes are getting bigger, better, and less expensive. Here's a brief tour (Vignettes on these and many other mango-growing nations appear in Appendix I.):

Australia: By the mango's centennial year Down Under, more than half a million trees had been planted, the majority of them in the state of Queensland. In 1993, four government agriculture agencies in Australia began a rootstock breeding program in which 1,900 hybrid lines are being evaluated for use by Aussie mango growers.

Israel: The United States and several other nations, Israel and Australia preeminent among them, have engaged in rootstock and germplasm programs to help produce new, improved cultivars and better commercial mangoes. In Israel, the calcareous, high-pH soil is not conducive to growing mango trees, but mangoes have long been grown in the Gaza Strip. The first organized planting of mango trees took place in Jewish settlements in the early 1930s, after their introduction by Professor Otto Warburg. No one knows when the first trees were brought into the country, but most likely they came from

Egypt. Since 1933, cultivars from South Africa, Egypt, and the United States have been introduced, and in the 1950s, commercial cultivars from Florida arrived.

Thailand: Using a revolutionary close-spacing growing technique and raising significant numbers of off-season mangoes, Thailand is among the world's leaders in mango production and export.

Technical Specifications

*M*ango trees can grow to reach one hundred feet in height and can produce fruit for forty years or longer. Recent cultivars have been developed that allow apartment dwellers to raise small trees on their patios, decks, or balconies. The fruit borne by these dwarf trees is the same size as their full-sized counterparts.

Mangoes come in two varieties: the Indian type and the Indochinese or Philippine variety. The former has a monoembryonic seed, which produces the most brightly colored fruit. The brighter fruit, of course, is popular for sale to consumers. Indian mangoes are more curvaceous, tending toward a rounded or kidney shape, tapering elegantly toward the apex. The Indochinese or Philippine variety has a polyembryonic seed and produces a less exotically colored fruit that is less commercially desirable for fresh-fruit sales. It tends to be a long, slender, sometimes cylindrical fruit. It can range from light yellow to yellowish green when ripe.

Depending on cultivar, the fruit can range from plum-sized varieties, such as the Kalmi and Chandrakaran, to tasty varieties of about half a pound, such as the Zill, to the whoppers, such as the Keitt and Kent, which may top the scales at two or more pounds each.

From the time blossoms appear on the panicles to the time the fruit is ripe for picking ranges from approximately 90 days for early-season varieties to 190 days for late-season types. Each of the panicles produces from about three hundred to more than seven thousand tiny blossoms, but only a small percentage become pollinated and produce tiny buds. Once the buds reach nubbin size, many drop well before maturity due to premature ripening, wind, rain, or other climatic conditions.

Say the word "mango" and many of us think of the fruit with vivid, luscious orange flesh. In truth, though, mango flesh can range from white (such as the Ice Cream), to a greenish yellow (such as the Brooks), to the more common orange. The Kesar mango from India is green-skinned but has red flesh when ripe. Thailand's Tong Dum mango is nicknamed "Black Gold" because its dark green skin appears almost black when ripe, but the fruit's inside flesh is a vibrant, golden hue.

Suppliers tailor the varieties they sell to fit their clients' tastes. Indians, Egyptians, and Southeast Asians, for example, prefer ripe, fiber-free mangoes with yellow skin. Many Thais and other Asians often consume their mangoes while the fruit is still green. African, European, and American consumers tend to prefer ripe mangoes with a red or orange blush on the fruit's shoulder.

The Mango Family Tree

Mangifera indica is the mango's scientific name. It comes from the family *Anacardiaceae*, whose seventy-three-member family tree is as bizarre as the Addams family's. Forty-one plants thrive in the *Mangifera* species, and seventeen of them bear edible fruit. Among the mango's distant relatives are the Jamaica plum, pistachio, and cashew, but so are poison ivy and other similarly toxic plants. The Brazilian pepper (*Schinus terebinthifolius*), also called the Florida holly, is a distant relative too. Like the mango, the Brazilian pepper is not native to south Florida, but after its import, the plant found the soil and climate optimal for proliferation. On the West Coast, the peppertree (*Schinus molle*) is a popular landscape shrub in southern California.

Relatives *Mangifera sylvatica* (wild mango), *Mangifera foetida* (horse mango, or bacang), *Mangifera odorata* (kuini), *Mangifera verticillata* (bauna), and *Mangifera panjang* (membangang) are generally smaller and more fibrous than their hifalutin cousin, *Mangifera indica*. They also usually have a seed that is proportionally larger to the size of the fruit and have a good bit more sap. Otherwise, they are similar in taste (though sometimes more sour), and all are consumed in a variety of ways. Here are some facts about these and other mango varieties:

- Membangang are grown on Borneo in the Brunei Darussalam, Sarawak, and Sabah areas. Membangang have a tougher outer skin than the mango, but the orange interior flesh is similar.
- The bacang (or bachang) is native to Vietnam and Malaysia.

- The kuini (or kuwini) also is indigenous to Malaysia.
- The bauna is grown in the Philippines and has, over the years, been considered for commercial use. Its fruit is rich and juicy and has a lovely aroma.
- The wild mango is grown in many places, notably in Nepal, on the Andaman Islands and in forests near Assam in northern India, in the Chittagong Hills in Bangladesh, and in Orissa in eastern India. The wild mango is very similar to *Mangifera indica* in many ways, though its shape is not as rounded and curvaceous as its cultivated cousin, except for cultivars such as Totapari, Nang Klang Wan, and Nam Doc Mai, which also taper to a point.
- *Mangifera zeylanica* grows in Sri Lanka. The small fruit is remarkably mangolike, although the tree's foliage and blossom panicles differ from those of *M. indica.*
- Other edible members of the *Mangifera* clan include *M. altissima* (pahutan), which is native to the Philippines. *M. laurina* (water mango, or manga-monjet), a plum-sized fruit imported to the United States in 1990, is native to Java, Borneo, and Malaysia. Finally, the inferior-tasting *M. caesia* (binjal) is native to Java and Sumatra.
- There's also a non-relative pretender, *Irvingia gabonenesis* (bush mango), native to Cameroon and the forests of West Africa, which is also being studied for possible commercial possibilities. Like *M. indica*, the bush mango is a giving tree with good-tasting fruit and wood used for timber.

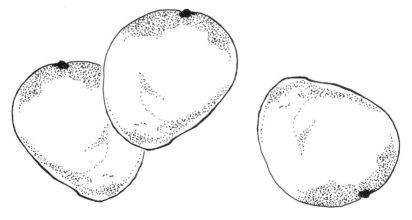

Wholly Nutritious, Batman!

No matter its coloring or variety, a ripe, medium-sized mango provides carbohydrates, fiber, Vitamins A, B_1, B_6, and C, sodium, calcium, magnesium, zinc, copper, manganese, iron, phosphorus, potassium, pantothenic acid, and niacin. In all, the mango has about 35 calories and a hint of fat, but not a whisper of cholesterol.

The mango's ties to poison ivy and Brazilian pepper help explain why some folks tend to break out (or have more serious reactions) when they touch the fruit or the sap or when they eat the fruit. A substance in the sap, the thin, white liquid (called *am ki chep*) that sometimes squirts from the stem as it is separated from the fruit, is the culprit, causing a severe allergic reaction in some people. Many people who suffer from this allergy (called *mango dermatitis* or *rhus dermatitis*) may continue to enjoy eating the fruit—they just can't touch it. (They can use a fork, don gloves to peel the fruit, or have someone else do it.) As a group, compounds, oils, and saps from *Anacardiaceae* probably cause more contact dermatitis than any other plant group. Additionally, some mango cultivars are also likely to cause diarrhea, particularly very ripe and fibrous fruits.

Mango Nuptials

*A*mong Indians, many of whom are Hindus, plants have a special role in sacred rituals. Lord Krishna, for example, is said to have a home within the tulsi plant, and its leaves—as well as those of mango, coconut, and banana plants—are important in Hindu *pujas*, or prayer rituals. The average Indian, if pressed to pick a national symbol for good fortune, would most likely choose the lancelike mango leaf. Not only is the fruit adored and beloved in India, in some cases the tree is too.

Planting mango trees is a deeply spiritual act that bestows grace upon the planter and also brings him responsibility for the tree. Like a dutiful parent, the planter's responsibility is at its greatest when it comes time for the tree to marry.

That's right, marry. An enduring tradition (though not a very common one) in India, and one certainly of immense curiosity to Westerners, is the symbolic marriage of trees. When the planter's tree or grove of trees reaches fruit-bearing age (in the case of mangoes, as early as age three or so for grafted trees and age six to eight for plants grown from seed), tradition forbids adults to partake of the fruit until the tree (or grove) is properly married. The mango marriage, like marriage among humans, is bound by tradition and ritual. The tree is symbolically considered the daughter of its planters, and the marriage to another plant is usually arranged by its "parents." A Brahmin officiates, and the trees are joined by thread or twine. A tree is married only once, no matter how many times "she" bears blossoms.

The usual suitor for a mango tree is a tamarind tree. The tamarind produces a small brown fruit whose sticky interior is used to flavor sauces. If a tamarind tree is not available near the mango tree, a jasmine may be used. If no other suitable trees are available, a wooden stake or the carved figure of an adult male may stand in for the groom.

The ceremony varies by area, but each mango marriage usually involves anointing the mango tree at its base with some vermilion paste. The happy "parents" may also be anointed. Ritual gifts such as sugar, flour, and rice are offered in a small sacrificial fire, which is fueled by clarified butter, called ghee. Prayers are recited and ritual foods are consumed.

What's a good wedding without a reception afterward? After the formal ceremony, the party begins. The parents' neighbors and friends are invited, and for the first time, they may partake of the first fruits produced by the tree. These auspicious, happy events often involve several hundred guests and put the proud parents into deep debt.

In some areas, mango trees or others, such as banyans or banana trees, are regarded appropriate suitors for wells or tanks. The well or tank is considered the male partner in the union, and each benefits from the other. The well provides water (or the tank stores it) so the tree may flourish; the tree provides good fortune so the water will continue to flow. Other symbolic weddings with mango trees may be performed with women who wish to bear children or with males or couples before their actual wedding.

The mango also has a place of importance in human marriage in India too, since it bestows the triple whammy of good luck, fertility, and longevity. In ancient times, when the groom, along with his family and entourage, traveled to his future wife's home for the marriage ceremony, stopping to rest in mango orchards along the way was considered wise. In modern times, the groom's father creates a ropelike garland made of bound mango leaves to hang outside his son's home for the wedding. The groom may also elect to tie a mango leaf to his wrist before the wedding and remove it after he and his new bride move into their home.

But maybe you're a skeptic and all this discussion about mango marriages and sacred symbolism seems like so much mumbo-jumbo. Just how pervasive can the allure and importance of a fruit be, for heaven's sake? Good question. Consider the twenty-seven-year-old woman in Kesarpura, India, who lifted her *ghungat* veil long enough to gobble down some mango she had purchased in the local market. Someone reported the indiscretion to her husband, who beat her severely for flouting local tradition. Ashamed, she swallowed poison and died.

II

Using Mangoes

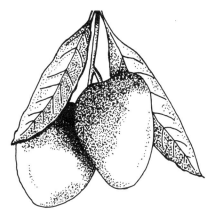

A Mango Owner's Guide

The Many and Varied Uses

The mango's flavor is delicate, subtle, and thoroughly intoxicating. There are few acts in life sweeter, messier, and more fulfilling than peeling a ripe mango and eating it ravenously, allowing the sweet juice to cascade down one's face and neck. Among mango devotees, the joke goes, the best place to eat mangoes is in the bathtub—buck naked.

For the more socially conscious mango lovers among us, the three-pronged mango fork is available to keep messiness to a minimum. It uses a long, sharp center tine to pierce the seed and two smaller tines at the sides to help stabilize the fruit so that it may be eaten as though it were a large, luscious lollipop.

The fresh fruit has star quality, and any mango maniac can attest that the best way to eat it is to chow down on chilled fresh mango with nothing more than a little fresh lime or lemon juice on it. How else may the mango be served? Let us count the ways:

- Frozen
- Pureed
- Dried
- In juices, nectars, and other beverages
- Preserved in cans
- In jams, jellies, pastes, preserves, and marmalades
- In pickles, relishes, salsas, and chutneys
- In salads and salad dressings
- In main courses, particularly as a sauce
- In candies and other confections, such as *li hing* mango, a

Hawaiian treat of dried mango slices dusted with a sweet/sour/salty preserved plum powder that islanders and *haoles* alike crave

❧ In *amchur* (also called *amchoor* and *aamchur*), a powder made from dried mango, popular among people from India and used in a wide variety of dishes

❧ As green mango nubbins, the immature fruit, popular in some Asian cuisines

❧ As mango kernel oil, one of six tropical oils (along with palm, illipe, kokum guri, sal, and shea oils) that may be added in the manufacture of milk chocolate

❧ As a Japanese dish in which tender young mango leaves are steamed and eaten with rice

The mango truly is a giving tree, and its uses are not limited to foodstuffs. Some other uses for parts of the mango tree include these:

❧ In Hawaii and India, craftsmen fashion mango wood into clocks and other attractive items such as picture frames, jewelry boxes, and rocking chairs. Mango timber is also used in boat and home construction. The wood, which ranges in hue from pale yellow to light greenish gray, is prized for its variable grain and dramatic flecks of orange and green that sometimes streak through it.

❧ Mango wood is considered the sacred wood of choice for Indian fire-walkers, and for religious and symbolic reasons, it is the wood of choice in many funeral pyres in India as well.

❧ In Kenya, authorities are urging wood carvers to use plentiful varieties, such as mango and neem, to help lessen demand for mpingo and muhugu trees, which are being decimated.

❧ In India, families festoon their doorways with mango leaves after the birth of a child to announce their happy news. Among Christian Indians, mango and banana trees are often selected for decoration during the Christmas season.

❧ Many Hindus ritually clean their teeth on holy days with brushes made of bundled mango twigs. Twigs also are used as firebrands for sacred fires of Homa and other religious occasions.

* Some parts of the tree, most notably the blossoms and leaves, are used in the preparation of pharmaceuticals, ranging from lotions to soothe hemorrhoids to medications to end hemorrhaging and clear up nasal problems, cardiac conditions, and menstrual disorders. Mangoes are also popular in a wide variety of folk medicines. One example is an Indian paste made of cooked mango, mint, ground cumin seeds, salt, pepper, and sugar. The paste is then diluted with water and drunk to prevent sunstroke.
* The sap is used as an adhesive, the bark is used to make dyes for tanning leather, and the fibrous husk around the kernel is ground and used as an additive to animal feeds.
* The oil pressed from the kernel is used to make soap, emollients, and other aromatic and skin care products, as well as cooking oil used in Africa.
* The fiber from the tough outer casing of the kernel is used in the manufacture of fine brushes, and the soft inner kernel can be dried and ground into meal that is used to make cereals.

Is it any wonder that in ancient Sanskrit writings the mango was called *kalpa-vriksha*, the wish-granting tree?

Slicing Mangoes

For some reason, there seems to be some dispute over the best way to slice mangoes. Because the mango is asymmetrical, some folks find it difficult to slice. Unlike apples, pears, and such, you'll never get nice even cuts, but no matter. You can still slice them or cube them without turning them to mush.

The simplest way to slice a mango is this:

1. Peel the mango
2. Rinse it in cold water
3. Slice the flesh away in spears lengthwise, following the contour of the fruit

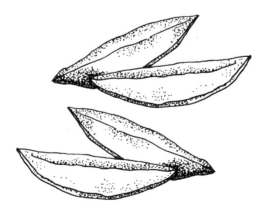

Or with a deliciously ripe mango, you can just slice through the meat along the two long, flat sides of the seed and scoop the flesh out with a spoon. Others prefer to make mango hedgehogs and cube the flesh off:

1. Using a sharp paring knife, slice each side of the unpeeled mango along the flat side of the seed, which will leave you with two fleshy halves and a seed, which you can discard.
2. Place one half of the mango with the cut side up on a cutting board and score the mango deeply, taking care not to cut all the way through the skin.
3. Use your fingertips to bend the outer peel backward so the chunks stand away and you may easily trim them from the peel.

If you're enjoying green mangoes Thai style or cooking with green mangoes, you can simply use a vegetable peeler to remove the skin. Softer, ripe mangoes require a sharp knife for peeling.

Some varieties, such as the small, stringy Kalmi or the tiny Chandrakaran, don't really lend themselves to slicing. Indians call these varieties "sucking mangoes." They're best enjoyed when ripe by washing the outside of the chilled fruit, then rolling it firmly between the hands to bruise the flesh and break the fibers inside. When the fruit is soft and juicy, cut a nickel-sized hole in the top of the fruit and simply suck the juice out. Be sure to wash your hands and mouth after finishing the mango.

Storing and Freezing Mangoes

For folks who live in the prime mango-growing areas of the U.S., the "season" runs from May through August in Hawaii and May through September in Florida. During those months, our trees are groaning with luscious, fragrant fruit. Tree owners learn who their friends are and, in a growing number of instances, who their enemies are too. Tree owners watch with amusement or anger as folks hop over their fences in the dead of night to pick windfall mangoes off the ground, or as the culprits scamper up trees to shake fruit from the branches. Some even return home to find their trees stripped bare.

But most of the time, particularly in abundant years, tree owners find themselves lugging bags and boxes of fruit to work, to friends' homes, even to the local homeless shelters and soup kitchens. In Hawaii, tree owners often place a box at the edge of their property and fill it with mangoes for their shy neighbors. Tree owners hate to see the fruit go to waste when they have more than they can eat themselves.

Time is of the essence when mango season arrives. Most mangoes are eaten fresh and ripe, and even if you start out with hard-as-a-rock ones, their shelf life is a week at best, often less. Using them before they spoil requires speed, planning, and some flexibility.

Some folks avoid freezing mangoes because they say the fruit turns to mush when it's thawed. While the thawed fruit is indeed a bit softer, it doesn't have to be mushy. An excellent way to freeze mangoes is to slice them and dip them in a bath of limeade or lemonade. Place the slices, not touching, on cookie sheets that have been sprayed with nonstick pan coating. Place the cookie sheets in the freezer and allow the fruit to freeze solidly. Later, release the slices by using a spatula and place the pieces in freezer bags with resealable closures. This way, you may use as many slices as you need and return the rest to the freezer. Serve the mango slices when they are mostly but not completely defrosted.

Another way to store mangoes is to puree them, pour the thick liquid into small freezer bags, jars, or even ice cube trays, and freeze them. If you enjoy using mangoes for beverages, shakes, mousses, or baked goods, you may find this an excellent alternative to the slice-and-freeze method. A squeeze of lime juice in the puree helps bring out the flavor.

If you don't live in a mango-growing area but are fortunate enough to receive mangoes as a gift, leave them out at room temperature in a light, warm area (such as a windowsill) for a few days. When the fruit's flesh responds to slight thumb pressure, it's probably ripe. Ripe fruit may be stored in the refrigerator for a few additional days. Cold fruit is easier to slice too.

Thanks to advances in propagation, shipping, and storing methods, mango lovers everywhere can get their favorite fruit throughout the year. Mango growers go to all sorts of lengths to ensure the quality of their product. In one region of the Philippines, for example, the fruits are wrapped in paper as they are picked. Also, they are picked between 9 A.M. and 3 P.M. to avoid getting excessive chep (sap) on the fruit when it is separated from the stem.

One of the most glorious things about mangoes is their aroma. Aromatic fruit is tastier, but fruit that's shipped green never really gets the chance to develop properly, so while you may end up with a tasty fruit, you don't get to savor the scent or taste to the max. If you're buying mangoes in the supermarket, try to select fruit that has a blush of red, orange, or yellow. Give it a sniff too up at the stem end. If you can smell that rich, sensuous aroma, so much the better. If it has all the bouquet of freshly dug potatoes, try again another day.

GREEN WITH (MANGO) ENVY

Using Green Mangoes

*M*ost mango lovers in the Americas prefer to eat their mangoes ripe. There are only a few green mango dishes that appeal to the North American palate, including chutneys, green mango pie, and a few salads. In Asia and the Pacific Rim countries, mangoes are far more likely to be consumed well before they ripen.

In Thailand, for example, the ripe mangoes on display at sidewalk stands look especially inviting because merchants impale them with an ice cream stick and carve the fruit's flesh into designs to increase their consumer appeal. It's marketing at its most basic, but it's effective. Still, the sour, acidic taste of the green mango appeals more strongly to the Asian palate. The same Thai mango monger who's carving the ripe fruit so he can sell it before it rots happily sells green mango spears with a choice of dipping mixes to his regulars. Among the topping faves are salt, which blunts the acidity; a mixture of granulated sugar and ground red pepper; and a mixture of soy and hot pepper sauces.

In addition to chutney, which originated in India, other Asian and Pacific mango favorites include fresh salads, mango pickles, relishes, and a variety of other dark, turmeric-laced dishes such as *thokku* and *gojju*. The Nam Doc Mai mango, from Thailand, is probably the most popular of the green-eating mangoes. Other popular varieties include Brooks, Cedar Bay, Duncan, Falan, Gaylour, Golek, Gow, Hong Sa, Ivory, Kaimata, Keow, Keow Savoey, Lebmue Dam, Lin Ngo Hou, Maha Janka, Mun, Nan Klang Wan, New Guinea Long, Ngot, Nong Sang, Nuwan Chan, Pim Saen Mun, Rad, Saiphon, Sungi Siput, Tekin, Tong Dum, Tuong, and Xoai Tuong.

III

Mango Recipes

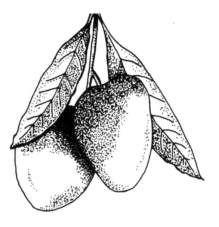

Serving the World's Most Popular Fruit

Appetizers and Salads

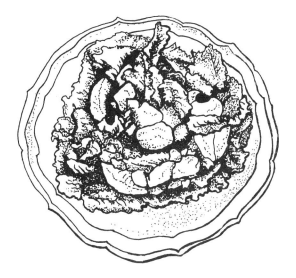

We Floridians eat pretty lightly, especially during mango months. Here are a few light, easy-to-make salads and appetizers.

Coconut Shrimp with Mango-Lemon Dip

This tasty combination makes a great party platter. It also makes a pound of shrimp stretch a long, long way.

FOR THE DIP:

8 ounces lemon yogurt

1 cup ripe mango, pureed

1 tablespoon lime juice

FOR THE SHRIMP:

1 pound white shrimp, shelled, deveined, and rinsed

Milk

1 cup grated, sweetened coconut flakes

1 cup panko (Japanese bread crumbs)*

2 eggs, beaten

3 cups canola oil

Mix dip ingredients together in a bowl and refrigerate to chill. Prepare the shrimp and soak for 10–20 minutes in a shallow bowl filled with just enough milk to cover them. Mix together coconut flakes and panko in a shallow casserole or pan suitable for breading.

Dip each shrimp in egg, coat with panko-coconut mixture, and drop into hot oil. Fry until each piece is golden brown. Remove from oil and allow to drain completely on paper or drying rack.

Arrange shrimp on a platter with bowl of dip in the middle and provide long toothpicks. *Fills one small serving platter (approximately 12 inches in diameter).*

Panko is readily available at Japanese groceries and many Asian groceries, but if it's not available in your area, you can use white bread crumbs as a replacement. If you can get the panko, please do. It makes for superior coconut shrimp.

Grand Avenue Mango Salad

Each summer, the Goombay Festival, a Bahamian arts, entertainment, and cultural extravaganza, is held along Grand Avenue in Miami's Coconut Grove. Traditional Bahamian foods are a big part of the fun. Along with chick peas and rice and conch salad is this easy-to-make mango dish.

2 small to medium green
   mangoes, peeled and
   sliced
salt and pepper
apple cider vinegar

Place mangoes in a flat-bottomed glass dish, such as a small casserole. Add salt and pepper to taste. Add enough vinegar to cover the slices and refrigerate for several hours before serving.

Las Olas Seafood Salad

Las Olas Boulevard is Ft. Lauderdale's chi-chi shopping and dining street, running from the beach west to the intersection of the Riverfront at Andrews Avenue. To their credit, chefs on Las Olas (which, by the way, means "the waves" in Spanish) have discovered the beauty of the mango and use it in many dishes.

1 cup fresh leek, finely sliced (Use the white portions of the stalk, not the more bitter green portion.)

2 plum tomatoes, sliced and seeds removed

1 small to medium mango, peeled and sliced or cubed

1 small jar marinated artichokes, cut into bite-sized pieces

1 6- to 8-ounce package of crab meat (artificial crab meat may also be used)

Juice of 1 lime

1 tablespoon sesame oil

1 tablespoon sesame seeds

Fresh salad greens

1 avocado, peeled and sliced

Several pinches of pico seco

FOR PICO SECO:

1/2 cup salt

1/2 cup crushed red pepper, finely ground

1 teaspoon ground cayenne pepper

1 teaspoon ground black pepper

1 teaspoon ground white pepper

Place all ingredients except salad greens, avocado, and pico seco in a nonmetal mixing bowl and toss together lightly. Combine pico seco ingredients in a shaker jar and mix well. Line serving plates with salad greens and arrange salad mixture in center of each plate. Place sliced avocados on top of salad mixture and sprinkle a pinch of pico seco on each. *Makes four side salads or two main-dish salads.*

Mango-Prosciutto Rollups

If you've tried melon-and-prosciutto rollups and loved them, this easy, elegant, and exceptional appetizer is about three rungs up on the taste bud ecstasy ladder. The prosciutto's saltiness and the mango's gentle sweetness play off each other perfectly. Try this recipe and you'll eschew melon as prosciutto's preeminent accompaniment forever.

1 medium to large ripe but firm mango
Juice of 1 lime
1 pound prosciutto, sliced paper thin
Long, frilled toothpicks

Slice mango lengthwise into long, thin spears about 1/2 inch wide by 1/4 inch.

Place spears in a nonmetal bowl and squeeze lime juice over them. Wrap each slice with prosciutto and secure with a decorative toothpick. *Makes 24 to 36 rollups.*

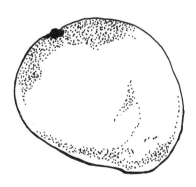

Pineapple-Mango Slaw

This is a little twist on an old favorite. Mom's simple and simply delightful dressing brings out the flavor.

FOR THE SALAD:

4 packed cups shredded green cabbage

1/2 cup diced mango

1/2 cup diced pineapple

1 small jalapeno pepper, finely minced and seeds removed

2 ounces raisins (optional)

FOR THE DRESSING:

1/2 cup mayonnaise

1/3 cup sweet pickle juice

1/4 cup cider vinegar

dash of salt and pepper

Mix all slaw ingredients well. Prepare dressing, drizzle over slaw ingredients, and mix well again. Refrigerate for about 30 minutes before serving. *Makes 8 servings.*

Troppo Fruit Salad

"Troppo" is how Australians say tropical. You'll feel as though you've "gone troppo" with this light, zesty fruit salad. This recipe makes a huge bowl, suitable for feeding eight to twelve at a beachside party or family picnic.

2 cups mango, peeled,
  rinsed, and cubed
1/2 cantaloupe, cubed
1/2 honeydew melon, cubed
1 cup fresh pineapple, rinsed
  and cubed
1 cup red or white seedless
  grapes, rinsed and stems
  removed
1 kiwifruit, peeled and sliced
6 strawberries, rinsed and
  halved
1/4 cup macadamia nuts,
  minced
1/2 cup orange juice
Juice of 1/2 lime
1/4 cup sweetened coconut
  flakes

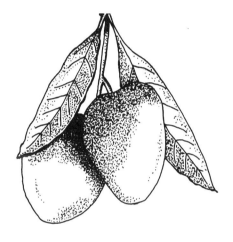

Mix all ingredients together except lime juice and coconut. Squeeze lime juice over salad and sprinkle coconut on top just before serving.

Summer Seafood Salad with Sesame-Mango Champagne Dressing

This main-dish salad requires a lot of ingredients, but this is a wonderful dish to serve the family for a light luncheon.

FOR THE DRESSING:

2 ounces extra virgin olive oil

4 ounces champagne vinegar

4 ounces champagne or sparkling white wine

2 tablespoons honey

1 teaspoon chopped fresh chives (Freeze-dried ones are acceptable in a pinch.)

1 teaspoon fresh mint, finely chopped

2 ounces mango puree

Juice of 1/2 lime

FOR THE SALAD:

8-ounce package mixed baby greens

8-ounce package crab or lobster

8-ounce package frozen salad shrimp, defrosted, drained, and rinsed

1 small can mandarin oranges, drained

1 cup bean sprouts

1 tablespoon sesame seeds

2-ounce package slivered almonds, toasted

2 plum tomatoes, sliced

1 ripe avocado, peeled and sliced into strips

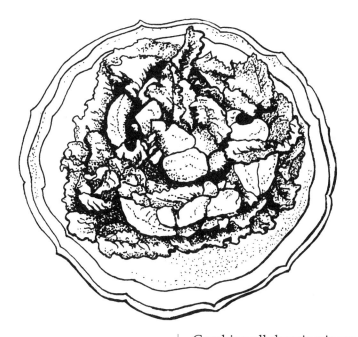

Combine all dressing ingredients in a bottle, shake well, and refrigerate. Make a "nest" of baby greens on each plate. Toss together seafood, oranges, bean sprouts, and sesame seeds. In the center of each nest of greens, place dollop of seafood mixture and top with toasted almond slivers. Artfully arrange tomatoes and avocado slices along edge of each plate and drizzle with dressing. *Makes 4 servings.*

Yaam

In Thailand, a special variety of mango is grown for this salad, but you can use just about any green mango, provided it is not too sour-tasting. The mango you select should have reached its full size but should not have started to lighten or soften.

1 medium to large green mango, julienned

1/2 cup cashew halves, toasted

1/2 cup peanut halves, toasted

1 cup thinly sliced purple onion

1/2 red bell pepper, sliced into strips

1 tablespoon sesame oil

1 tablespoon soy sauce

1 11-ounce can mandarin oranges, drained

1 tablespoon sesame seeds, toasted

1 teaspoon dried red pepper flakes

1 teaspoon Japanese mixed pepper powder (optional)*

In a large bowl, place together all ingredients except sesame oil, soy sauce, mandarin oranges, sesame seeds, and dried red pepper flakes. Mix sesame oil and soy sauce and drizzle over mixed ingredients; then add mandarin oranges and toss until mixed. Sprinkle with sesame seeds and red pepper flakes before serving.

*For an extra special kick, add the mixed pepper powder, which can be found in Japanese groceries under the name Nanami Togarashi, made by S&B Foods. A 15-gram bottle costs about $2.50. The special punch it adds to the dish makes it worth the extra effort. It doesn't produce the kind of heat that pepper lovers crave but does give this novel salad zip and pep.

Mango Entrees

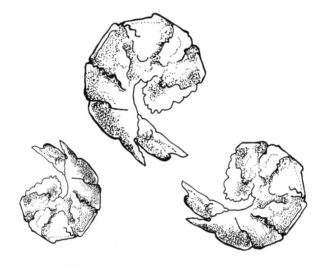

Mangoes add a special taste to chicken, fish, shrimp, and pork dishes. Enterprising cooks also use it successfully with other types of seafood and with beef.

Chicken Stir-fry with Mangoes and Asian Corn

This is an easy-to-make weekend family meal that also makes a good outdoor meal for entertaining. Prepare all the ingredients ahead of time, use your wok on the gas grill, and whip this dish up in no time.

1/4 cup olive oil

3 chicken breasts, cut into thin strips

1 red or orange bell pepper, sliced into strips

1 green bell pepper, sliced into strips

1 can Asian baby corn

1 tablespoon sesame oil

1/4 cup pineapple juice

1/4 cup light brown sugar

1 tablespoon cider vinegar

1 tablespoon soy sauce

1 tablespoon cornstarch mixed with 1/4 cup cold water

1 medium mango, firm but ripe, sliced lengthwise into spears

4 teaspoons sesame seeds, toasted

Pour olive oil into heated wok or saute pan, add chicken strips, and turn chicken until nicely browned on all sides. Remove chicken and set aside. Add peppers, Asian corn, and sesame oil to cooking pan. Allow vegetables to cook quickly until they become slightly tender. Then add pineapple juice, sugar, vinegar, soy sauce, and cornstarch in water. Add mango and browned chicken. Allow to cook until chicken is fully cooked and mango turns tender but not mushy. Divide mixture among 4 plates and sprinkle teaspoonful of toasted sesame seeds over each dish.

Grilled Chicken with Pineapple-Mango Salsa

2 pounds chicken tenders or sectioned chicken breasts

FOR THE MARINADE:
12-ounce bottle Naranja Agria
Splash of soy sauce
Splash of extra virgin olive oil
Splash of Louisiana-style hot sauce

FOR THE SALSA:
1 medium onion, diced
1 cup mango, diced
1 cup fresh pineapple, diced
1/2 ounce fresh cilantro, roughly cut
Splash of extra virgin olive oil (optional)
1 teaspoon minced fresh ginger

2 tablespoons minced fresh garlic
1 small Scotch bonnet or jalapeno pepper
3 or 4 chopped fresh mint leaves
Juice of 1/2 lime

Combine marinade ingredients. Add chicken, mix, cover, and refrigerate, allowing chicken to marinate for about an hour. Combine salsa ingredients except lime juice. Mix well. Grill chicken, top with the salsa, and squeeze lime juice over salsa before serving. *Makes 6 servings.*

*Naranja Agria is a sour orange sauce that makes a fantastic marinade. You can buy it at your favorite Hispanic grocery.

Grilled Pork Chops with Mangoes

With a nice hot fire and thinly cut pork chops, your time spent over the hot grill will be minimal. The coconut topping takes just a minute to make beforehand.

2 pats butter

1/4 cup sweetened coconut flakes, toasted

1/4 cup panko (Japanese bread crumbs)*, toasted

8 thinly sliced pork chops, marinated for several hours in mojo criollo**

8 mango halves, peeled (Use fruit that is ripe but still firm.)

Olive oil

*You can buy panko at Asian or Japanese markets, but if it's not available, you can use regular white bread crumbs in a pinch.

**Mojo criollo (usually just called mojo) is a Spanish marinade and barbecue sauce made of water, vinegar, onions, garlic, and spices.

While you're building your fire, melt butter in a small pan, add coconut and panko, and stir until all butter is absorbed. Remove from burner. Place pork chops on grill, then mango halves (which you may want to moisten with a bit of olive oil beforehand).

Grill chops until done. Grill mangoes several inches from coals, turning regularly, until flesh begins to soften. Don't allow them to blacken, but make sure they get a good tan. Sprinkle coconut mixture over mangoes and serve with pork chops. *Makes 4 servings.*

Islander Chicken

My brother, Joe, thought this one up while he was fishing in a billfish tournament in the Bahamas. He needed a one-pan dish that was elegant, tasty, and easy, and this fits the bill. We've eaten it many times since, and it seems to get better each time we make it.

1 bottle Chablis wine
3 boneless, skinless chicken breasts, quartered
4 ounces butter
4 large garlic cloves, crushed
1 cup orange juice
2 tablespoons soy sauce
1/4 teaspoon cinnamon
2 medium mangoes, peeled and sliced lengthwise into spears

Pour Chablis into a large skillet. On high heat, poach chicken breasts in wine for about seven minutes. Reserve one cup of liquid and pour off and save remainder. Add butter and garlic to pan and slowly pan-fry chicken until brown and completely cooked. Return reserved liquid to pan and add orange juice, soy sauce, cinnamon, and mangoes. Cover and simmer for 10 minutes. *Makes 4 servings.*

Last Key Shrimp Kabobs

This is a great main course for a beach cookout. Not your run-of-the-mill picnic fare, it's easy to prepare in advance and doesn't take up much room in the cooler!

1/4 cup honey

1/4 cup dark rum

Juice of 1 lime

1/4 cup melted butter

Wooden skewers soaked for one hour in water

1 pound fresh shrimp, shelled, deveined, and rinsed

1 medium ripe but firm mango, peeled and cut into chunks

1 pound fresh pineapple chunks*

Dissolve honey into rum and lime juice and pour in melted butter. Cut each skewer to about 10 inches and load with shrimp, mango, and pineapple. Make sure each kabob starts and ends with a shrimp—it'll tighten on the skewer and keep the fruit from slipping off.

Grill as close to coals as possible, only long enough to cook shrimp thoroughly. Baste kabobs frequently with honey mixture. *Makes 16 to 18 kabobs.*

You can usually buy bags or containers of precut pineapple cubes. They're a great timesaver.

Accompaniments

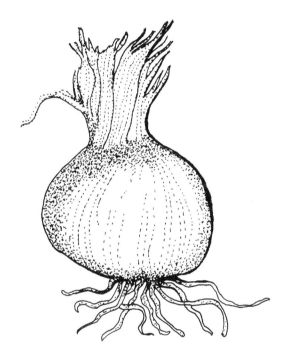

Mangoes are great stars of the picnic or dinner table, and they're also exquisite character actors. Here are three excellent sides. A fourth, pineapple-mango salsa, is located in the Main Events section with grilled chicken on page 45.

Bes' Kine Mango Salsa

It's quick and simple to prepare, and it's simply the best salsa I've ever tasted on grilled chicken breasts, fish, or pork chops.

1 cup mango, diced

1 small yellow onion, diced

3/4 teaspoon crushed red pepper

1/4 red bell pepper, diced

1 tablespoon olive oil

Juice of 1 lime

In a mixing bowl, combine first four ingredients. Top with olive oil and lime juice and mix. Serve immediately. *Makes enough to accompany four main courses.*

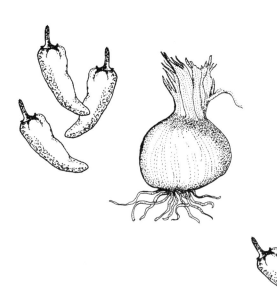

Mango Mexicana with Pico Seco

*Got a lonesome-looking piece of grilled pork, chicken, or fish
that needs a zesty sidekick? Try mangoes the spicy way many
Mexicans love them.*

Mangoes, peeled and sliced

1 lime, sliced

Healthy pinch of pico seco

Sesame seeds (optional)

FOR PICO SECO:

1/2 cup salt

1/2 cup crushed red pepper,
  finely ground

1 teaspoon ground
  cayenne pepper

1 teaspoon ground
  black pepper

1 teaspoon ground
  white pepper

Combine pico seco ingredients in a
shaker jar and mix well. (In addition
to giving mangoes zest and zip,
pico seco goes well on fruits such
as papaya and melons. It's also
wonderful atop fresh green salads,
corn, cucumbers, jicama, and more.)
Arrange 3 to 4 mango slices on each
plate with meat or fish entree,
squeeze lime section over mango,
and sprinkle pico seco on top.
Sprinkle sesame seeds on top if
desired. *Makes 4 servings.*

Mexican Mango-Jicama Salsa

Looks aren't everything. The mango is a gorgeous, seductive fruit that exudes a luscious aroma and tastes even better than it smells. But pity the poor jicama (pronounced HIK-uh-muh), an ugly duckling of the vegetable world, looking vaguely like a potato with an overabundant waistline. And that's a shame too, because those who know the jicama lovingly refer to it as the "apple of the tropics." Once you cut it, peek inside, and take a bite, you'll see it has a crisp, crunchy, radishlike interior with a taste that's an alluring cross between water chestnuts and apples.

In Mexico, the jicama is used as widely as the potato is in the United States. The salsa recipe that follows combines several ingredients much loved by Mexican cooks and, with its light taste and interesting texture, makes a zippy accompaniment for chicken, fish, or pork.

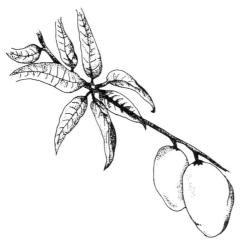

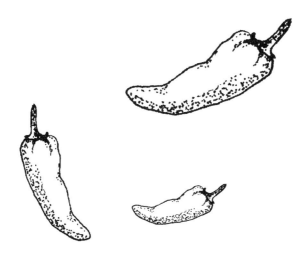

1 cup jicama, diced

2 tablespoons cilantro,
   cut roughly

1 teaspoon dried crushed red
   pepper or minced fresh hot
   pepper (preferably
   Jamaican bonnet peppers)

Pinch chili powder

Juice of 1 lime

1 cup ripe mango, diced

Place mango, jicama, cilantro, and pepper together in a bowl. Sprinkle chili powder and drizzle lime juice over the mixture and toss until ingredients are well mixed. Serve immediately. *Makes 4 servings.*

Desserts

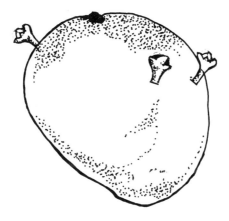

The sweet yet light taste of mango goes perfectly in desserts, particularly uncooked ones. In fruit salads and other mixed-fruit desserts, mangoes are the consummate team players. Here are a few suggestions, but feel free to experiment.

Sticky Rice with Mangoes

Budbod ug mangga *is the Philippine name;* kao new ma muang mun *is its Thai name. Whatever you call it, this is a well-loved dessert that helps settle the digestion, takes the edge off a fiery main course, and is a snap to make.*

One word of advice: Don't confuse coconut milk with coconut cream. Coconut cream is exceptionally sweet and is used to make piña coladas and other similar drinks. Coconut milk can usually be found in the ethnic foods section of your local supermarket or at specialty foods stores.

14-ounce can coconut milk

1/2 cup sugar

1/2 teaspoon salt

1/4 cup light raisins

1 cup long-grain white rice, cooked and cooled

1/4 teaspoon cinnamon

Dash nutmeg

2 cups mangoes, cubed

Whipped cream

In a saucepan, combine coconut milk, sugar, and salt. Stir with a wire whisk on low heat until mixture is smooth. Add raisins and cook gently for about 10 minutes. Remove from heat. Add coconut mixture to rice. Add spices and stir thoroughly. Chill well. To serve, spoon rice mixture into serving cups, then cover with layer of chopped mangoes and dollop of whipped cream. *Makes 6–8 servings.*

Mango Mousse

1 package orange gelatin

1/2 cup boiling water

1/2 cup sugar

8 ounces heavy whipping
  cream

1 cup mango puree

8-ounce package cream
  cheese, softened to room
  temperature

Mix gelatin with water. Add sugar and stir until dissolved. Put mixture in refrigerator or freezer. In mixing bowl, whip cream until almost stiff. Refrigerate. Place mango puree and softened cream cheese in blender and blend until smooth.

When gelatin has cooled but has not yet begun to gel, use blender or wire whisk to mix gelatin into whipped cream, then fold in mango–cream cheese mixture. Blend thoroughly but gently. Spoon into individual serving cups or pour into mold and chill completely. *Makes 6–8 servings.*

Spiced Stewed Mangoes

Goes nicely atop vanilla, coconut, or other tropical fruit–flavored ice cream.

3 cups water

2 green mangoes, peeled and sliced

1 cup sugar

2 or 3 cinnamon sticks

1 teaspoon whole allspice

6 whole cloves

Place all ingredients in saucepan and bring to a boil. When boiling begins, reduce heat so mixture can boil very slowly for about 40 minutes or until it begins to thicken. After thickening begins, remove saucepan from heat and pour liquid through strainer. Reserve liquid. Remove fruit from spices; then pour fruit and reserved liquid into a jar. Cover and refrigerate. *Makes 4–6 servings.*

Summer Fruit Salsa

This is a simple dessert that makes use of bountiful summertime fruits and is elegant enough to serve to guests. It also makes a delightful picnic dessert. Note: Make sure all fruit is firm but ripe.

1 angel food cake

FOR SALSA:

1 medium mango,
  finely diced

1 nectarine or peach,
  finely diced

1 apricot, finely diced

1 purple plum, finely diced

1/4 cup sweetened,
  shredded coconut

1 shot Triple Sec

FOR TOPPING:

1/2 cup heavy whipping
  cream

2 tablespoons confectioners'
  sugar

1 teaspoon vanilla

Place all fruit in medium bowl. Add coconut and mix gently until all fruit is evenly distributed throughout mixture. Drizzle Triple Sec over mixture. Cover bowl with plastic wrap and refrigerate for several hours.

Whip cream, sugar, and vanilla until firm. Cut angel food cake into one-inch slices. Smother with fruit salsa and top with hefty dollop of topping. *Makes 4–6 servings.*

Mango-Pineapple Drop Cookies

I'd been tinkering with a mango cookie recipe for ages but never got to first base with the idea, much less scored. One night while I was making trail mix with dried fruit, it came to me: use preserved fruit. But how to bring the flavor out and keep from breaking a tooth on baked preserved fruit? I'd been feeding my little boy some prunes that weekend and had been thinking about making fruit compote. Another revelation: I decided to cut the preserved fruit into tiny pieces, pour boiling water over them, and allow them to soak for just one minute to soften them but not long enough to wash all the flavor out. The result looked good, so I whipped up a huge batch of cookie batter and added my favorite cookie ingredients.

The first tray I overcooked, but still the cookies had a great flavor. I couldn't wait for the second batch to turn golden brown. I took them off the tray and allowed them to cool. They looked good. They smelled great. Now, if only. . . . It was Sunday night and I was watching TV. As soon as prime time ended, I sprinted into the kitchen and grabbed a cookie. It was wonderful. I wanted to have my husband try one, give one to my son, but at 11 P.M. on a Sunday? Of course not. So Monday morning I packed a container of them for my mom and dropped them off at her house. She called just before noon.

"Don't ever bring those cookies here again," she told me sternly.

"Why?" I asked, suddenly crestfallen.

"I can't stop eating them," she said. "I have to finish them now. Goodbye."

2/3 cup dried mango,
   minced
1/3 cup dried pineapple,
  minced
Boiling water
1 stick butter, softened to
   room temperature
1 packed cup light brown
   sugar
1 egg
1 1/2 cups all-purpose flour
1/2 teaspoon baking soda
Pinch salt
1/2 cup macadamia nuts,
  roughly cut
2/3 cup sweetened,
  shredded coconut
  (I prefer Angel Flake.)

Preheat oven to 350°. Place mango and pineapple in small bowl and add boiling water, just enough to cover fruit. Let water remain on fruit for one minute; then pour off water and place fruit in large mixing bowl. Add remainder of ingredients and mix thoroughly. Drop walnut-sized gobs of cookie dough onto greased pan and bake until golden brown (about 15 minutes). *Makes 4 dozen.*

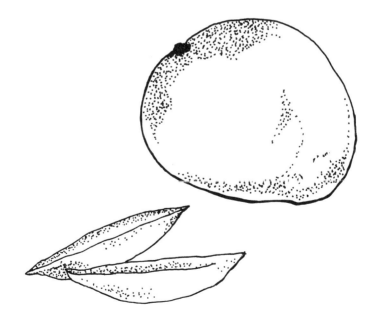

Upside-Down-Under Cake

This is a mango upside-down cake made with an Australian sponge cake called a Lamington.

FOR THE TOPPING:

2 small ripe mangoes, sliced

Juice of 1/4 lime

6–8 maraschino cherries, sliced

1 cup light brown sugar

FOR THE CAKE:

3/4 cup sugar

1 3/4 cups self-rising cake flour

1 cup sweetened, shredded coconut

3 teaspoons vanilla extract

1/2 cup milk

3 eggs

3/4 cup melted butter

Preheat oven to 375°. Thoroughly grease a 9" x 13" baking pan and cover bottom with mango slices. Drizzle lime juice and sprinkle cherry slices and brown sugar over mangoes. Set aside.

Blend all dry cake ingredients. Add vanilla, milk, eggs, and melted butter. Mix until all ingredients are thoroughly blended and gently pour mixture over fruit in baking pan. Bake for about 45 minutes or until inserted toothpick comes out clean. Allow to cool for a few minutes; then invert cake onto flat-bottomed serving platter and allow to cool thoroughly before serving.

Wikiwiki Fresh Fruit Dessert

Wikiwiki *in Hawaiian means "in a hurry," so if you need a delicious, healthy dessert in a flash, this one hits the bull's-eye. Seasonal berries also work nicely in this dish.*

1 cup mangoes, cut into chunks

1 cup fresh pineapple, cut into chunks

1 cup papaya, cut into chunks

1 cup bananas, cut into 1/2-inch slices

Juice of 1/2 lime or lemon

1 cup orange yogurt

Toss fruits with lime or lemon juice and drain off remainder of liquid. Fold yogurt into fruit mixture and serve. *Makes 4–5 servings.*

Nonalcoholic Drinks

Mango drinks don't need alcohol to give them extra appeal. Here's a selection of mango-based, nonalcoholic beverages that have real pizzazz.

B Sting

*The smooth, light taste of this juice drink makes it delightful.
The whopping dose of beta-carotene makes it good for you too.*

6 cups water

2 cups orange juice

1 small to medium carrot,
   juiced

1 small peach, peeled and
   pureed

3/4 cup ripe mango, pureed

3/4 cup sugar (or equivalent
amount of artificial
sweetener)

Juice of 1 lime

Blend all ingredients, strain,
and chill well before serving.
Makes about 1/2 gallon.

Mango Milkshake

Batido *is one of the Spanish words for "milkshake." (The other is*
licuado.) *Traditionally, Hispanics make their milkshakes thin.
For a more Hispanic taste, add a bit more milk to the recipe
as you see fit.*

8 ounces milk

1/2 pint vanilla ice cream

1/2 medium mango, cut
   into chunks

1 teaspoon vanilla extract

1 dash nutmeg

Place all ingredients except nutmeg
in a blender and blend well.
Pour into glasses and dust top
of each drink with nutmeg.
Makes 2 servings.

Mango Milkshake with Cream of Coconut

Cream of coconut is a smooth, rich, sweet addition to many Caribbean and Hispanic dishes and turns an ordinary milkshake into an event. Make sure you use coconut cream, not coconut milk, which is unsweetened.

6 ounces milk

2 ounces coconut cream

2 tablespoons sugar

1/2 medium mango, cut into chunks

1/2 pint vanilla ice cream

1 teaspoon vanilla extract

Toasted shredded coconut

Place all ingredients except coconut in a blender and blend until smooth. Pour into glasses and sprinkle top of each drink with toasted coconut. *Makes 2 servings.*

Gardner's Punch

Working in the yard in summertime has mixed rewards. The plants are at their most beautiful and abundant during this time, but the heat is oppressive and taking frequent fluid breaks is a must. This light, tasty punch helps you replace the fluids and many of the nutrients you sweat away. Served in a tall glass with lots of ice, it's a tiny oasis.

4 ounces fresh pineapple, cut into chunks

4 ounces mango, cut into chunks

1 cup watermelon, seeds removed, cut into chunks

1/2 cup orange juice

4 heaping teaspoons sugar

1 ounce lemon or lime juice

5 cups water

Place all ingredients except water in a blender and liquefy. Transfer to a large pitcher or punch bowl, add water, and stir. *Makes 1 pitcherful.*

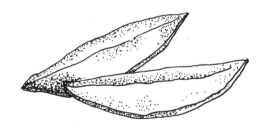

Mango Juice

When young Cuban balsero *(rafter)* Elián Gonzalez *was rescued clinging from an inner tube off the coast of Florida, rescuers took him to Memorial Medical Center in Hollywood. The six-year-old's first request at the hospital was for a glass of his favorite beverage, mango juice. Although you can buy canned mango juice and nectar, there's nothing like the real thing, made fresh and served icy cold.*

1 cup ripe mango, pureed
4 cups water
1/2 cup sugar
Juice of 1/2 lime

Pour mango puree into a pitcher or carafe; add water, sugar, and lime juice, and stir until sugar is dissolved. Refrigerate and serve cold. *Makes 1 quart.*

Some folks prefer to strain their mango puree to get the tiny flecks of mango pulp out. I prefer to leave them in. It's all a matter of taste.

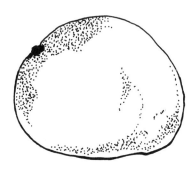

Mango-Orange Frost

My mom's always on a diet and has concocted some truly delicious recipes that are low in fat and high in fiber. This is one of them.

2 medium mangoes, cut into slices and frozen

2 cups orange juice

2 packets of artificial sweetener

8 ice cubes

Place mangoes, orange juice, and sweetener in a blender and blend well. Add ice cubes one at a time until fully blended.
Makes 4 servings.

Miss Mattie's Front Porch Cooler

Miss Mattie was my maternal grandmother. Like any good child of the South, she liked her recipes quick and easy to make so she could scoot out on the porch and gossip with the relatives who seemed to visit every summer. (One way to be sure you'll see a lot of your relatives is to move to Florida.) This is a recipe of hers that I tinkered with a bit. A strict Southern Baptist, she would surely want me to point out that the optional vodka was among my ideas, certainly not hers.

Small can orange juice
  concentrate
1 cup mangoes, pureed
2 1-liter bottles 7-Up
Vodka, to taste (optional)
Maraschino cherries
Lime or orange slices

Mix orange concentrate, mangoes, and 2 cups of 7-Up in a pitcher. Pour mixture into ice cube trays and freeze. Place 4–5 cubes in a tall glass and fill with remaining 7-Up. Add vodka, if desired. Garnish with maraschino cherry and lime or orange slice. The remaining frozen cubes may be turned out of the trays and stored in plastic bags in the freezer until needed, making them easy to use for future parties or picnics. *Makes 2 trays.*

Traditional Lassi

Lassi is a yogurt drink that is popular throughout India. Its texture is the same as a milkshake, but many folks prefer it a bit thinner.

1 cup plain yogurt
1/2 medium mango, cut into
 cubes or chunks
6 ice cubes
2 tablespoons sugar
Juice of 1 lime wedge

Place all ingredients in a blender and blend until smooth.
Serve in tall glasses with straws.
Makes 2 servings.

Tropical Lassi

A new twist on an old favorite.

1 cup plain yogurt
8 frozen mango cubes*
2 tablespoons honey
1/3 cup unsweetened apple
 juice

Place all ingredients in a blender and blend until smooth.
Serve in tall glasses with straws.
Makes 2 servings.

*Mango cubes are made by pureeing ripe mangoes, adding a little lime juice, pouring mixture into ice cube trays, and freezing.

Whitecap Tropical Freeze

4 ounces water

2 ounces mango, cut into chunks

2 ounces fresh pineapple, cut into chunks

Juice of 1/2 lime

Sugar or artificial sweetener to taste

2 tablespoons nonfat milk powder

12 ice cubes

Sweetened, shredded coconut

Maraschino cherries

Place all ingredients except milk powder, ice, coconut, and cherries in a blender. While blending, add milk powder slowly to avoid making lumps. After milk has been whipped in thoroughly, add ice cubes one at a time.

Spoon mixture into tall glasses and serve with a long-handled spoon and a straw. Sprinkle a little coconut and a maraschino cherry on top of each drink as a garnish and serve. *Makes 2 servings.*

Alcoholic Drinks

Could anything possibly murmur "Florida" better than frothy, frosty, pastel-colored drinks served poolside in tall glasses with little umbrellas? Bartenders love mangoes for a variety of reasons. The puree adds body and subtle sweetness to drinks. The juice provides an exotic change from commonly used mixers. And you can't beat a ripe slice of mango skewered with a maraschino cherry and a pineapple chunk as a garnish in any tropical drink. Mango's flavor also partners exceptionally well with coconut, banana, orange, lime, lemon, and guava.

Mango Colada

A piña colada with mango. What could be more refreshing?

6 ounces coconut cream

6 ounces pineapple juice

4 ounces mango puree

4 ounces spiced white rum

8 ice cubes

Place all ingredients except ice in a blender and add ice cubes one at a time. Blend until smooth. *Makes 4 servings.*

Frozen Mango Daiquiri

4 ounces mango puree

3 ounces white rum

Juice of 1 lime

1/4 cup sugar

Ice cubes

Place all ingredients except ice in a blender. Blend thoroughly until mixture is smooth and sugar is dissolved. Add ice cubes one at a time and blend to desired consistency. *Makes 4 servings.*

Frozen Mango Margarita

4 ounces white tequila

4 ounces lime juice

4 ounces Triple Sec

1/2 cup mango, cut into chunks

2 teaspoons sugar

12 ice cubes

Lime juice

Salt

Place all ingredients except last two in a blender and blend until smooth. Coat the rims of 4 oversized martini glasses with lime juice and salt; pour margarita mix into glasses.
Makes 4 servings.

Mangria

It's simply sangria with mangoes. Simply delicious too.

2 clementines, peeled, separated, and broken

1 medium mango, cut into medium-sized chunks

1 cup white seedless grapes, halved

Juice of 1 lime

Juice of 1 orange

1 bottle Lambrusco wine

Place all fruit in the bottom of a glass pitcher and mix well. Add lime and orange juices and wine. Cover and refrigerate several hours before serving. Spoon a little of the fruit mixture into each glass before pouring the wine in.
Makes 1 pitcherful.

A Trio of Mango Shooters

Let's be adults about this now. Shooters, by their nature, are small drinks that carry an uncommon wallop and often contain a strange mixture of liquids. Most folks drink them just for the kick. What sets these mango shooters apart is that they're designed for taste and don't use a lot of bizarre ingredients. Don't drink them on an empty stomach. Go easy and savor the taste—and be sure you have a designated driver to get you home safely.

The base ingredient in each of these recipes is Coco Lopez Mango Drink Mix, which is tough to find. If you can't find it, mix mango juice with the juice of one lime wedge and a tablespoonful of sugar and use as a substitute.

BAY STREET BLAST

1/4 cup Coco Lopez Mango Drink Mix (or substitute)
1/4 cup cream of coconut
1/4 cup Nassau Royale liqueur
1/4 cup crème de banana

Place all ingredients in a shaker filled with crushed ice. Shake, strain, pour, and serve. *Makes 4 servings.*

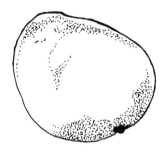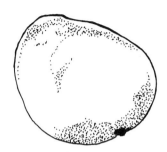

KEYS SUNSET

1/4 cup Coco Lopez Mango
  Drink Mix (or substitute)
1/4 cup cream of coconut
1/4 cup DeKuyper Key Largo
  Tropical Schnapps
1/4 cup 151-proof rum
Grenadine

Place all ingredients
except grenadine in a
shaker filled with ice.
Shake, strain, pour into a
tall shot glass or Russian
vodka glass, and top with
a drop or two of grenadine
just before serving.
Makes 4 servings.

SUNSPOT

1/4 cup Coco Lopez mango
  drink mix (or substitute)
1/4 cup 151-proof rum
1/4 cup Cointreau liqueur
1/4 cup Alize de France

Place all ingredients in
a shaker filled with ice.
Shake, strain, and
pour into glass.
Makes 4 servings.

Mariposa

The name is Spanish for "butterfly." This frosty drink goes light on the tongue.

2 ounces white rum
1/2 very ripe banana
1/2 medium mango, cut into chunks
2 ounces coconut milk
1 teaspoon vanilla extract
2 tablespoons sugar (or equivalent amount of artificial sweetener)
1/2 pint vanilla ice cream
6 ounces milk

Place all ingredients in a blender and blend until smooth. *Makes 2 servings.*

Icy Treats

In the midst of a sultry, steamy summer, two things bring instant relief: jumping into the ocean or a swimming pool, and eating frozen fruit pops. In Britain, they're called ice lollies. Not all of us have access to a suitable body of water, but we can all treat our own bodies to a variety of frozen fruit pops with mango as a starring or supporting ingredient. Frozen fruit pops can be made in ice cube trays or in paper cups, but they look so much more delectable when frozen in ice pop molds. Housewares outlets and discount department stores often carry them during early summer.

The easiest kind of mango ice pops is too simple to include as a recipe. Simply make a pitcher of your favorite limeade or lemonade and stir in a cup of pureed mango. Pour the mixture into pop molds and freeze. The citrus juice contributes vitamin C and the mango adds a nice dose of vitamin A. If you use artificial sweetener, you can cut down on the calories.

Children love these, but they may have to beat the adults to the freezer for them!

Athlete's Punch Pops

If you've been out rowing, running, or just roaming in the heat, a frozen pop especially hits the spot. This recipe offers a true tropical taste and provides lots of vitamins, minerals, phytochemicals, and other things that are good for your body.

16-ounce bottle of Citrus
  Cooler Gatorade
4 ounces guava nectar
8 ounces pureed mango
Juice of 1 lime wedge
2 tablespoons sugar

Blend all ingredients well, pour into pop molds, and freeze.
Makes about 16 frozen pops.

Cherry-Mangoberry Frozen Fruit Pops

2 ounces bing cherries,
  stones removed
2 ounces blueberries
2 ounces strawberries
2 ounces mangoes
2 tablespoons sugar
8 ounces water
Juice of 1/2 lime

Blend all ingredients well, pour into pop molds, and freeze.
Makes about 8 frozen pops.

Mango-Coconut Ice Lollies

Coconut water (also known as agua de coco) *is a mixture of the liquid inside coconuts, young coconut meat, sugar, water, and preservatives. It comes in soda-sized cans and has a mildly sweet coconut taste. Popular in the Hispanic community and available at most Latin markets, it is often drunk straight from the can. The coconut and mango complement each other well, and the tiny flecks of coconut meat are an added plus.*

1 can coconut water
1 cup mango puree
1/3 cup sugar
Juice of 1 lime

Blend all ingredients well, pour into pop molds, and freeze. *Makes about 16 frozen pops.*

Kulfi and Kulfi Kones for Kids

Kulfi is a summery alternative to ice cream that originated in India. It requires no cooking and is quickly and easily made, and children positively adore it.

FOR THE KULFI:

3/4 cup mango, pureed

Juice of 1/4 lime or lemon

1/4 cup sugar

1 box pineapple gelatin

Boiling water

5 ice cubes

1/2 pint heavy whipping
 cream

FOR THE KULFI KONES:

Sugar cones

Shredded coconut, sprinkles,
 or other similar nonpareils

Mix mango puree, lime or lemon juice, and sugar and set aside in the refrigerator. Dissolve gelatin in 1/2 cup boiling water. Add five ice cubes and stir until cubes are dissolved. Refrigerate until gelatin gels. Whip cream with a hand blender until it begins to form soft peaks. Add gelatin and mango mixture to cream and whip until cream stiffens. Be careful not to overwhip and cause cream to break down. Place mixture in freezer. Serve frozen. *Makes 8–12 servings.*

To make kulfi kones, spoon kulfi into sugar cones just as it begins to freeze. The mixture should be stiff enough so you can build a nice head on the cone. Sprinkle coconut or sprinkles on top of kulfi and place cones upright in juice glasses.

Place glasses in freezer. Once cones are fully frozen, removed them from glasses, wrap in plastic, and stored in freezer until served. *Makes 10–12 cones.*

Mango Granita

This is so simple to make, it's sinful. The taste is icy and refreshing—a summertime treat that can't be beat.
Children like it as much as or maybe more than adults do.

1 quart limeade or lemonade

1 medium mango, liquefied

Make quart of your favorite limeade or lemonade, using fresh limes or lemons. (Make mixture a bit on the sweet side.) Pour limeade or lemonade into ice cream maker along with mango. Freeze according to manufacturer's instructions and enjoy. *Makes about 10 servings.*

Note: If you remove the slushy mixture and place it in your freezer, it hardens into a lovely Italian ice.

Thai Ice Pops

If you've ever had Thai iced tea, you'll notice how coconut milk adds a richness and smoothness to the tongue. This recipe does the same to a mango ice pop.

12 ounces pureed mango

4 ounces water

2 ounces unsweetened coconut milk

Juice of 1 lime wedge

4 tablespoons sugar (or equivalent amount of artificial sweetener)

8 ounces orange juice

Blend all ingredients well, pour into pop molds, and freeze. *Makes 12–15 frozen pops.*

Mango Miscellany

A fruit as versatile as the mango blends into a variety of recipes. Here are a few recipes that don't quite fit into any of the other categories.

Mango Leather

Here's a wonderful fat-free, easy-to-make treat that makes a super lunchbox addition. Adults find it interesting too.

1 medium mango, sliced
2 tablespoons sugar
   (or equivalent amount of
   artificial sweetener)
Juice of 1/4 lemon
Pinch ground nutmeg
Pinch cinnamon

Preheat oven to lowest setting (usually 150°). Place all ingredients in a blender and puree. Cover bottom of a small cookie sheet or pizza pan with plastic wrap and pour mixture onto wrap.

Using a spatula or rubber scraper, spread mixture evenly. To reduce drying time, mixture should be no thicker than 1/4 inch at its thickest point, preferably less.

Place pan on middle shelf in oven. Allow mixture to remain in oven until it dries and reaches a rubbery consistency. This can take 10 or more hours depending on thickness of mixture and individual ovens.

After mixture has dried, remove pan from oven and pull fruit leather from plastic wrap. Using kitchen shears, slice leather into long strips about 1 inch wide. Roll strips and place them aside to cool and set. Wrap in plastic before packing in lunchboxes. *Makes 12–16 leather rolls.*

Mango-Nut Bread

Yes, it has a gazillion ingredients, but after a decade or so of tinkering with the recipe, this is the most delectable, delicious mango-nut bread I've ever tasted. It makes for wonderful luncheon finger sandwiches when filled with whipped or honey-nut cream cheese. It also is delightful when served à la mode as a dessert.

1 ripe banana

1/2 cup butter, softened to room temperature

3/4 cup light brown or turbinado sugar

1 cup ripe mango, cut into small cubes

2 cups unbleached all-purpose flour

1 teaspoon baking soda

1 tablespoon lime juice

1/4 teaspoon salt

1/4 cup chopped macadamia nuts

1/4 cup chopped pecans or English walnuts

1/4 cup sliced almonds

4 ounces honey

peel of 1 kumquat, sliced thinly (optional)

2 eggs

Preheat oven to 375°. Mash banana in a mixing bowl and add remaining ingredients, stirring thoroughly. Pour into two lightly greased loaf pans. Bake until golden brown and an inserted toothpick comes out clean. *Makes 2 loaves.*

Robbie's Spicy Ham Glaze

This is one of my mom's recipes. You'll find its lively, spicy taste plays well on a beautifully baked ham.

Ham

1 1/3 cups pureed mango

1/3 teaspoon ground cloves

3/4 teaspoon ground
 cinnamon

6 ounces honey

2 ounces orange juice

Preheat oven to 350°. Place ham in an open, uncovered baking pan. Blend all glaze ingredients and spoon glaze onto ham until its visible surface area is covered. Bake for 30 minutes or until ham reaches degree of brownness desired. Feel free to add more glaze during baking. *Makes enough glaze for one large ham.*

Mango-Poppy Seed Vinaigrette Dressing

This dressing works especially well on a salad of mixed greens, avocado chunks, and Maui (or Vidalia) onion rings.

2 ounces extra virgin olive oil
4 ounces cider vinegar
Dash salt
Dash garlic powder
Dash pepper
Splash Louisiana-style
  hot sauce
4 ounces pureed mango
1 tablespoon poppy seeds
4 teaspoons sugar
  (or equivalent amount of
  artificial sweetener)
Juice of 1/2 lime

Place all ingredients in a covered bottle and shake thoroughly.

Tropical Trail Mix

This recipe makes enough to feed your average Scout troop or the carload of kids you're carting around on a field trip. It's natural and provides a nice mix of carbohydrates, protein, and some fat for short- and long-term energy.

1 1/2 cups unsalted roasted peanuts, shells and skins removed

1 cup each of the following:

Dried mango, cut into small pieces

Dried cranberries

Dried pineapple, cut into small pieces

Chopped dates (Buy the pre-chopped kind.)

Roasted sunflower seeds

1/2 cup each of the following:

Roasted pumpkin seeds

Dried cherries or blueberries

Macadamia nuts, roughly chopped

Blend all ingredients well and divide among individual zip-lock plastic bags. (Keep stirring mixture because pumpkin and sunflower seeds will quickly settle to bottom.)
Makes 18 1/2-cup servings.

Ono Ono Tropical Bagel Spread

Ono ono *means "very very good" in Hawaiian. This tasty bagel spread is a breeze to make and a delight to eat. It's also yummy on toast, hot muffins, and fruit breads.*

8-ounce package cream
   cheese, softened to room
   temperature
1/2 cup mango, diced
1/2 cup crushed pineapple
1/4 teaspoon cinnamon

Blend all ingredients well. Refrigerate until ready to use.

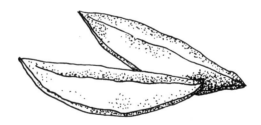

Recipes Online

Now that you've enjoyed some quick and easy mango recipes, here's your chance to get more adventuresome and try more esoteric and difficult dishes. Head to your computer, fire up your Internet browser, and you'll find thousands of mango recipes at your fingertips. Here are some websites mango lovers will find particularly fruitful.

The Tropical Fruit Growers of South Florida and the Florida Department of Agriculture and Consumer Services cohost a tropical fruits website that's truly superb. It's a place where mangoes get their due. You'll also find information on other interesting tropical fruits, from the common (banana, coconut, avocado, and Key lime) to the more exotic (wax jambu, jaboticaba, longan, mamey, and *monstera deliciosa*). Pay a visit at www.fl-ag.com/tropical.

* Will a thousand mango recipes satisfy you? Try www.freshmangos.com, which bills itself as "the world's largest mango recipe guide." There's no reason to disagree.
* A great place to search for cutting-edge, nouvelle mango recipes is The Food Network's website, www.foodtv.com.
* Southeast Florida's three dominant daily newspapers, *The Sun-Sentinel* (www.sun-sentinel.com), the *Palm Beach Post* (www-gopbi.com) and *The Miami Herald* (www.herald.com), do an outstanding job during mango season. Out West, the *Honolulu Star-Bulletin* does too. Call it up at www.starbulletin.com and enjoy excellent mango coverage by veterans Catherine Kekoa Enomoto, Betty Shimabukuro, and others. The *Star-Bulletin* covers the usual suspects, plus Hawaiian mango favorites such as Moki mango, crack seed (a curious dish of Chinese origin which is in no way cracked, nor does it contain seeds of any sort), mango pickles, *li hing* mango, and mango strips.
* The Recipe Archive at http://recipes.alastra.com/ often features mango recipes and gets more than thirty-five thousand hits daily. It's definitely worth a visit.
* You can find thousands of mango recipes from around the globe, spanning the mundane (salsas), the delightfully exotic (Tahitian mangoes in wine), and the downright scary (mango pesto and mango meatloaf), simply by typing in "mangoes" on your favorite search engine.

Appendix 1

MANGOES AROUND THE WORLD

Mango-growing Countries

Mangoes first began their spread throughout the temperate climates of the world with the help of peripatetic Buddhist monks. In the sixteenth, seventeeth, and eighteenth centuries, their proliferation came largely with the help of Portuguese traders, who spread them far and wide. Today, countries have elected to introduce mangoes as a commercial crop, with varying degrees of success. All the countries listed grow mangoes; countries with an asterisk export mangoes. This appendix, culled from archives and dozens of interviews with mango experts and mango lovers around the world, helps show the spread and popularity of mangoes and provides a few curious anecdotes and infobits.

Anguilla
Mangoes are among the native-grown fruits chosen for depiction on postage stamps. Most of the fruit is grown on the eastern side of the island. The fruits ripen from May to July.

Aruba

Antigua and Barbuda
A minimal number of mangoes are produced annually for commercial sale; the remainder are for local consumption.

Argentina*
Australia*
Mangoes were once thought to have been introduced in Australia around 1849 or 1850, possibly by a man named Bidwill, but a reference to the failure of experimental mango crops in 1837 was made in a Governor's Dispatch from New South Wales in 1838.

Regardless of the time of their introduction, mangoes are now among the country's favorite fruits and fruit crops. The state of Queensland produces eighty percent of Australia's national crop of mangoes; the Northern Territories produce fifteen percent. Western Australia continues to expand its market share, which was worth $2 million in 1991–92. Although mangoes are grown in Australia and the northern tip of New Zealand's north island, they are not grown on Tasmania.

Australia's national and state governments are making an ambitious effort to become a global leader in mango production, particularly with the Kensington Pride mango, which has been embraced by Asian consumers. A polyembryonic species, Kensington Pride was introduced from India by horse traders and first grown at Bowen, Queensland. In 1993, the National Mango Breeding Program was initiated to develop new hybrids, which have been entering the market at a steady pace. The fruit ripens from October through early March.

Azores Islands
Mangoes were introduced here by Portuguese traders by 1865.

Bahamas Islands
Mangoes were introduced to the Bahamas in 1951 and are grown as a backyard and commercial crop on the Out Islands and on the island of New Providence, where Nassau, the capital, is located. The fruits ripen from April to August and occasionally as late as September.

Bahrain
Bali
Bangladesh*
Barbados
Mangoes were introduced to Barbados

by Portuguese traders from Rio de Janeiro in 1742.

Belize
Mangoes were likely introduced to Belize by the Garinagu (also called Garifuna), a group begun with African slaves who escaped two wrecked Spanish slave ships near St. Vincent in 1635. The Garinagu blended in well with the local Arawak and Carib Indians, and the group proliferated on St. Vincent. By 1797, after they had sided with France in a conflict against the British rulers of the island, the Garinagu had been forcibly removed by the British and transplanted to Central America, particularly Honduras (in 1797), Belize (by 1802), and Guatemala. By 1880, the Garinagu were trading mangoes with the Mayas of Ishcalac in the Yucatan Peninsula.

Mangoes are cultivated throughout Belize but seem to thrive especially in the lower coastal areas of the country. Most of the fruits ripen from May to July.

Benin*
Bermuda
Although Bermuda is further north than the normal growing area for mangoes, the warm weather there permits their growth as a backyard crop.

Bolivia*
Borneo
Botswana
Mangoes grow well in Botswana, particularly in the northern part of the country, above the Tropic of Capricorn. They also grow well in the Kasane and Tuli Block area, particularly in the areas of higher elevation.

Brazil*
Mangoes were introduced to Brazil by Portuguese traders at Bahia in 1700. A quarter of the country's mangoes are

grown in the Sao Francisco Valley, in the states of Bahia and Pernambuco. Much of the fruit ripens from October to February, although mangoes are grown year-round in parts of Brazil.

Burkina Faso*
The fruit ripens from March to June.

Burundi

Cambodia*
Cameroon
Canary Islands
When Captain Cook arrived at Madeira in 1768, he found mangoes growing in abundance there.

Cape Verde Islands*
Cayman Islands
Central African Republic*
Chad*

Chile
Before 1982, most of the mangoes grown here were varieties from China. In 1982, Florida cultivars were introduced. Chile now produces mangoes year-round.

China*
Mangoes have been grown in China since the seventh century and now are raised in the extreme southeastern part of the country, in the sheng (provinces) of Guanxi, Guzhou, Yunnan, Sechuan, and Guangdong and on the island of Hainan. The main commercial mango is the Zihua, which accounts for eighty percent of production.

Colombia*
Florida cultivars have done very well here, as have local varieties Bianato and Asuka. The fruit ripens in May and June.

Cook Islands*
Cormoros Islands
Costa Rica*
The mango came to Costa Rica in 1796 and, with the later introduc-

tion of Florida cultivars, the country has grown to become a vigorous exporting nation, with much of the crop going to the United States, particularly after Hurricane Andrew destroyed most of southeastern Florida's mango trees. The fruit ripens from February to September.

Cuba*

Cyprus
Mangoes were introduced to Cyprus in 1982 by Costas Gregoriou, a horticulturist working for the Agricultural Research Institute in Nicosia.
Dr. Gregoriou grew seeds of the Rose variety he had brought from Trinidad. Since then, several cultivars have been added, including Kensington Pride from Australia and Tommy Atkins from the United States. The country's mango-growing areas are located in the southwestern coastal areas.

Democratic Republic of Congo*
Dominica*
Most of Dominica's mangoes are planted in the drier agricultural, coastal areas of the northwest and northeast parts of the island. Julie is the main variety grown for export. The fruiting season runs from May through August.

Dominican Republic*
The Dominican Republic's portion of Hispaniola is covered with one million hectares of wild mangoes. In the mid-1970s, cultivated varieties began to be introduced. The fruit ripens from May through July.

Ecuador*
Ecuador began exporting mangoes in 1989. The fruit ripens from October to February.

Egypt*
Mangoes were brought to Egypt from

India in 1825 and planted in the gardens at Shubra palace of King Mohamed Ali Pasha. They are grown in all twenty-seven of the country's governates—commercially in twenty-three of them—with the greatest concentrations of trees in Fayoum, Giza, Ismailia, Kalyoubia, and Sharkia governates. The fruit ripens from May to August. Many Egyptian trees tend to bear fruit every other year.

El Salvador*
The fruit ripens from February through September.

Ethiopia

Fiji*

Gambia*
The fruit ripens from April through July, although it can go as late as October.

Ghana*
Starting in the 1920s, Ghana has made several concerted attempts to grow a variety of cultivars in the Ejura district.

Greece*

Grenada
Mangoes probably were introduced to Grenada during the nineteenth century. A big favorite among the island's residents, the fruit is also exported to the United States, Canada, and England. The cultivars used for fresh sales are the Ceylon, Graham, Julie, and Peach. The Long and Rose varieties are exported green for processing.

Mango trees were planted as windbreaks in the cocoa- and banana-growing areas in St. Andrew's and Victoria Counties after the visit of Hurricane Janet. The fruit ripens from April through June.

Guadeloupe*
Guam
Guatemala
Mangoes ripen from March to June.
Guinea*
Guineabissau*
Guyana*
No records exist for when the first mangoes were brought to Guyana or who brought them, but clearly it was well before the abolition of slavery in 1834. It had been a common practice for sugar growers to plant mango trees on their estates, but later the trees were cut down when it was learned they were a popular food source for runaway slaves. In the 1880s, a botanical garden was established in Georgetown and efforts were made to expand the number of mango varieties, but the collection was later destroyed. Most recently, in 1973, nine local and twelve foreign plants were imported from Florida for propagation at the Ebini Crop Station on the Berbice River. The trees grew large but did not produce fruit. Approximately twenty more varieties were planted at Ebini in February 1974.

Currently, the districts of Essequibo, East Coast Demerara, East Berbice, Corentyne Coast, and Rapununi are the leading producers of mangoes. Two crops are produced annually: one ripens in June and July, the other from November through January.

Haiti*
Haiti ranks fourth among mango-exporting nations and, with the assistance of USAID, has added more than thirty thousand grafted mango trees since 1995 to increase the production of mangoes for export.

Many Haitian trees bear in two seasons per year, October to December and March to July.

Honduras*

The fruit ripens from February through September.

India*

The world's leading grower of mangoes, India produces about sixty-five percent of the world's crop but is not the world's leading exporter because so much of it is consumed domestically. Although the fruit is grown throughout the country, the leading production area is Uttar Pradesh. "Wild" mangoes, *Magnifera sylvatica,* grow in forests in Assam and near Orissa. The most popular mangoes in India are yellow-skinned and sweet when ripe with little or no fiber.

For more than forty years, India's agricultural scientists have worked on developing more and better mangoes. In 1998, scientists from the Indian Council of Agricultural Research announced the development of the first seedless mango.

The fruit ripens in Southern India from February to June and in Northern India from May through August.

Indonesia*

For Earth Day, a McDonald's restaurant in Jakarta gave away five thousand fruit tree seedlings, with mango seedlings among the four varieties distributed. Mangoes were among the six tropical fruits chosen in 1997 for a research and development program as Indonesia moves closer to a market economy.

Iran*

Mangoes are grown primarily in the southern part of the country in the provinces of Baluchestan, Hormozgan, Jiroft, and Sistan. The fruit ripens from July to September.

Israel*

It's unclear when mangoes were introduced to Israel, but the first trees were likely grown from seeds brought from Egypt by Professor Otto Warburg. The first organized planting of trees occurred in Jewish settlements in Palestine in 1929 and the early 1930s.

Using cultivation and harvesting methods they developed and perfected, Israeli mango growers raise trees that provide phenomenal yields, sometimes as much as ten times greater per acre than nations using more traditional methods. Prime growing areas are north of the Dead Sea and in the Galilee region. Mangoes here ripen from July to early October and sometimes as late as December.

Italy*

Mangoes have been grown experimentally by researchers in southern Sicily, where they were introduced by 1905. Although the trees grow well and flower annually, the fruit has difficulty ripening properly and the fruit that does ripen has a strong turpentine taste.

Ivory Coast/Abidjan*

Research on mangoes is going strong here, with more than 140 varieties being grown at a research station. The fruit ripens from March to July.

Jamaica*

Mangoes were introduced to Jamaica in 1782, when a French ship headed for Hispaniola from what is now Reunion was captured by Captain Marshall of the British ship *Flora.* The captive ship was taken to Jamaica, and its cargo of mangoes, cinnamon, jackfruit, and other fruits was unloaded and entrusted to the care of Hinton East, who maintained a private botanical garden at Gordon Town, nine miles outside Kingston. Other varieties were introduced in 1793 by Capt. William Bligh, who brought seventeen mango plants from the island of Timor four years after his ship, *Bounty,* was taken over by mutineers in the South Pacific near Pitcairn Island.

In 1869, John Peter Grant, the governor at the time, imported at least twelve varieties from India, including Bombay, which were cultivated at Castleton Botanic Gardens. In 1884 and 1898, other grafted varieties were imported from Martinique. Other introductions were made in 1905, and, as late as the 1960s, more than twenty more varieties from India were introduced.

The top production areas are in the lowlands on the northern side of the island at Lima and St. James and in the southern plains. The fruit ripens from April through August.

Java

Larger commercial mango-growing areas include the districts of Bangil, Gresik, Mojokerto, and Probolinggo on the eastern part of the island nation. The Javanese mango industry is built around the luscious red-skinned Gedong cultivar.

Kenya*

Although most mangoes must be grown in lowland areas, Kenya's Harries and Sabre varieties can be grown at altitudes up to six thousand feet.

Laos*
Lesser Antilles
Liberia

Madagascar*
Malawi*
Malaysia

Yellow-skinned varieties are the most popular here. The prime mango-growing regions are in the extreme north in the states of Perak, Perlis, Kelantan, and Kedah and in the south in Malacca, Sembilan, and Negeri. Backyard trees are grown throughout the country.

Mali*

The fruit ripens from March to July.

Martinique
Mauritius

Mangoes were introduced to Mauritius in the mid-eighteenth century, probably between 1750 and 1790, by a French botanist named Lejuge and a man named de Guignes, who brought them from Goa, India. The fruit ripens from November to February.

Mexico*

A Spaniard, Don Juan Antonio Gomez, is credited with introducing the coffee plant and the mango to Mexico early in the nineteenth century, although some experts contend the first mangoes arrived there on Spanish galleons from the Philippines in the late 1700s and Gomez added new varieties. Other varieties came from the West Indies during the early 1800s too.

Mexico has grown to become the world's leading exporter of mangoes. The fruit ripens from February through early October.

Morocco

Mangoes, called "mangues," have been grown in Morocco for about eighty years in the regions of Agadir and Kenitra. The fruits ripen from September through November. Morocco produces about 70 tons of mango annually and in 1999 imported 210 tons, principally from Mali, Guinea, Senegal, and the Ivory Coast.

Mozambique*

Myanmar (Burma)
The mango is easily the favorite fruit in Myanmar, the mango's homeland. Most of the cultivars are named after the grower who developed the variety. The fruit ripens from April through July.

Nauru
This tiny Pacific island nation, located between the Federated States of Micronesia to the north and the Solomon Islands to the south, is better known for its rich phosphate deposits than its agricultural products. Mangoes are grown here, along with coconuts, figs, and wild cherries. The prime mango-growing region is around the Buada Lagoon.

Nepal
Known for its towering peaks, Nepal is a mango-growing nation, producing the fruit in the Kathmandu Valley, foothills, river basins, and other lowlands. The fruit, called "aap," ripens in the spring.

Netherlands Antilles
The islands of the Netherlands Antilles (Curacao, Bonaire, Saba, St. Maarten, and St. Eustacius) are a welcome climate for mango growth. Mangoes are popular fixtures on the menu at local restaurants. Some varieties bear fruit three times a year.

New Zealand
New Zealand seems an unlikely place to grow mangoes, but the peninsula at the top of the North Island is blessed with a subtropical climate, making it a great spot for mango propagation.

Niger

Nigeria*

Niue
Mangoes, pineapple, papaya, and coconuts are the main fruits produced within the world's smallest self-governing nation.

Oman*
Once a fruit of minor importance in Oman, mangoes took on a new role in 1990, when the government began an initiative to change from a mango-importing nation to a mango-exporting one. The government assisted growers by providing thirty thousand seedlings annually, supplanting the yellow, sour local varieties of unknown origin with better-looking and better-tasting fruit. Mangoes ripen here from May through August.

Pakistan*
The province of Punjab is Pakistan's prime mango-producing region. The fruit here ripens from June through early October.

Palestine

Panama*

Papua New Guinea
Mango season in Papua New Guinea is from November to December, at the end of the dry season. In most places of the world, "mango madness" is a time for rejoicing but not here. When the fruit starts to fall, so does the rain.

Paraguay*

Peru*
Mangoes ripen from October to March.

Philippines*
Whether by missionaries, pirates, or both, mangoes reached the Mindinao region and the Sulu Archipelago by about 1450. Nearly 150 years later, travelers from Siam or the Dutch East Indies introduced them to other parts

of the country, including the island of Luzon and the Visayas region. Grafted varieties began arriving in the early 1900s. The mango has grown to become the national fruit of the Philippines, the world's seventh largest mango-producing nation. The leading production region is Ilocos, followed in order by Southern Tagalog, Central Luzon, Western Visaya, Cagayan Valle, and Southern Mindinao. The mango industry is built around the Carabao mango, which is sold as the "Manila Super." Almost ninety percent of the Philippines' mango exports go to Hong Kong, with Japan and Singapore also receiving significant amounts.

The Philippines are home to both the National Mango Research and Development Center in Guimares and the Mango Information Network, an Internet-based information service for mango growers and shippers. Mangoes ripen here from March to May.

Pitcairn and Norfolk Islands

Portugal

It seems appropriate that the mango's greatest promoter would grow some at home too. From at least the middle of the eighteenth century, mangoes have been grown here, but Portugal is not a player in international mango commerce.

Puerto Rico*

Brought by Portuguese traders, mangoes first reached Puerto Rico by about 1750. The south coast of the island is the prime mango-growing area. The fruit ripens from February through September.

Samoa (American Samoa and Western Samoa)

Called "mago," the mango is enjoyed in Samoa as a fruit and is also widely used as a medicinal plant for upper respiratory and oral infections, including gingivitis. Mangoes are also used for a variety of gastrointestinal disorders.

Senegal*

The prime mango-growing areas are the regions of Casamance and Tambacounda. Mangoes help provide a food source for many Senegalese during the pre-rainy season, before the grains and peanuts mature. Local custom decrees that hacking a chunk out of the trunk of a mango tree will encourage it to produce more blossoms. The fruits ripen in April and May.

Seychelles

Mangoes were introduced here about 1850. Since the late 1970s, the republic's ministry of agriculture has maintained field gene banks. The onslaught of development now threatens the fruit's existence, and fields containing many varieties have already been lost. With the assistance of experts from the University of Mauritius, the Republic of Seychelles has placed its entire germplasm program on computer.

Sierra Leone*

Solomon Islands

Somalia*

South Africa*

Mangoes were introduced to South Africa by Portuguese sailors before the turn of the seventeenth century. Commercial production of mangoes began in the early part of the twentieth century. The fruit ripens from November through April.

Spain*

Spain began exporting mangoes in 1985.

Sri Lanka*
St. Kitts and Nevis
Julie is the main mango variety grown in island orchards.
St. Lucia*
Hurricane David's visit to the island in 1979 was devastating to the mango industry, but mangoes have been a key part of the crop diversity program since. Graham and Julie are the main varieties grown for export. The fruits ripen from April through September with a peak period in June and July.
St. Vincent and the Grenadines*
Julie and Imperial are the main varieties grown for export. The peak mango season is May and June.
Sudan*
Suriname
Through the mid-1960s, mangoes were grown solely as backyard fruits. The Golek and Roodborstje varieties are the top pick for commercial production.
Swaziland

Tahiti
Mangoes, called "va popaa," were introduced to Tahiti in 1848. At least four of the paintings done by Paul Gaugin during his Tahitian period include mangoes.
Taiwan
Mangoes probably were introduced to the island by the Dutch when they occupied southern Taiwan between 1624 and 1661. Mangoes are Taiwan's second largest fruit crop after citrus. Approximately twenty thousand hectares are devoted to mango growing on the island, mostly in the south in the Tainan, Kaohsiung, and Pinton counties. The fruiting season normally runs from April to July but sometimes starts as early as February

and occasionally runs as late as mid-September.
Tanzania*

Thailand*
Mangoes have been grown in Thailand for thousands of years. Graphic references to the fruit go as far back as the stone tablet of King Ram Khamhaeng the Great of the Sukhothai kingdom more than seven hundred years ago. About 170 varieties are grown in Thailand, 10 of which are commercial cultivars. Most of Thailand's commercial crop is consumed domestically, and many of the country's choicest varieties are eaten green. Thailand is among the leaders in improving growing methods to increase yields and create the ultimate in tasty, fiber-free mangoes.
Tonga
No mangoes are grown for export in Tonga, but they are a popularly cultivated backyard crop and also are sold in local markets in the kingdom, including Tongatapu, 'Eua, Vava'u, Ha'api, and the Niuas. With the help of Peace Corps volunteers, about twenty Asian and Florida cultivars were introduced, but much of the research planting was destroyed by typhoons in the 1990s.
Trinidad and Tobago
Trinidad's small mango industry isn't adequate to supply the nation's taste for the fruit, so mangoes are imported from elsewhere in the Caribbean. Trinidad and Tobago are planting more acres of mangoes yearly. The fruit ripens from April through August.

Uganda
We've all heard of banana republics.

Yoweri Museveni, Uganda's president, has referred to his country as a "mango republic."

United Arab Emirates*
United States*

Mangoes have been grown in the United States since 1824, when Capt. John Meek brought them to Hawaii on the brigantine *Kamehamaha*. They first reached the continental U.S. in 1833, when Henry Perrine introduced them in the Miami area. They reached California in 1880 and Florida's western coast in 1885. U.S. mango consumption doubled between 1989 and 1994. Although New Age and Floribbean cuisine have helped popularize the mango, only about thirty percent of Americans have tasted the fruit. Asians and Hispanics living in the U.S. account for a significant percentage of sales.

Hurricanes Andrew and Georges significantly damaged commercial mango-growing areas in south Florida. The fruit ripens from May through September.

U.S. Commonwealth of the Northern Mariana Islands

The Chamorro word for mango is "manga." The fruit probably was brought to these Pacific islands from the Philippines. The fruit is consumed ripe as well as green with a dash of salt, hot pepper sauce, and soy sauce. A local specialty on Saipan Island is "koko," pickled green mangoes well laced with the local atomic bonnet peppers, all washed down with a cold bottle of beer to quell the flames.

Upper Volta

Vanuatu
Venezuela*

The states of Guarico, Cojedes, and Aragua are the leading mango-producing states. The fruit ripens from January through March.

Vietnam*

Most of the mangoes grown in Vietnam are in the southern part of the country, in the lowlands such as Binh Dinh, Phu Yen, and Khanh Hoa, and in the provinces along the Mekong River delta. The majority of the mangoes planted in the northern part of the country are in Son La and Lai Chau provinces.

Virgin Islands

Wallis and Futuna Islands

Mangoes are grown on these tiny South Pacific islands but aren't quite the luscious fruits found in neighboring Fiji and Western Samoa. The fruits are so fibrous, the locals call them "hairbrushed." Because many of the trees are old and very tall, the fruits often become bruised when they fall.

Yemen*

Mangoes were introduced here late in the eighteenth century. As of 1995, they ranked the sixth largest fruit crop in Yemen behind grapes, bananas, papayas, oranges, and dates. Five varieties of mangoes are grown here.

Zaire*

Appendix 2

HOW MANY MANGOES?

International Mango Cultivars

Thousands of local varieties of mangoes are grown throughout the world, but the official list of cultivated varieties (cultivars) is maintained by the International Mango Registrar, Dr. R. R. Sharma, of the Division of Fruits and Horticultural Technology, Indian Agricultural Research Institute in New Delhi. Before a cultivar is added to the list, complete physical characteristics and genetic information are compiled and catalogued to ensure the variety merits its spot in the registry.

13-1
Abbasi
Abe-Hayat
Abreu
Achar
Achar Pasand
Adams
Adonka Mamidi
Adurki
Afeem
Afonsa
Afonsa de Portugal
Afonsinha
Agarbathi
Aga Saheb
Agni
Agria-Kosha
Ahping
Ajod Sindhurio

Akhadya
Akhuras
Akirpalli Nalla Rasam
Akirpalli Thella Mamidi
Akuti
Ala Fazli
Albela
Alda
Alfazli
Alib
Ali Bux
Alice
Alipasand
Allen
Allipasand
Allumpur Baneshan
Almas
Alphan
Alphonse

Alphonso
Alphonso Batli
Alphonso Bihar
Alphonso Black
Alphonso Bombay
Alphonso Poona
Alphonso Punjab
Alphonso Rumi
Alphonso White
Aman
Aman Abbasi
Aman Angoori
Aman Khurd Buland
   Bagh
Amarafro
Ambajan
Ambalavi
Ambe Hrid
Ambe Javi

Ameergola
Amelie
Ametista
Amijivan
Amin
Amin Abdul Ahmed
　Khan
Amin-Daseri
Amin Dudhia
Amin Heera
Amin Ibrahimpur
Amin Khan
Amini
Amin Khurd
Amin Lal
Amin Mohammad
　Yunus Khan
Amin Pasand
Amin Prince
Amin Sahai
Amin Tehsil
Amlet
Amoury Polly
Amrapali
Amrita Bhog
Amrit Sagar
Amruthakalasa
Amrutham
Amrutharasayanam
Amyoo
Anabi Gola
Anandapuram
　Suvarnarekha
Anannas
Anannas Khas
Anar Dana
Anar Kali
Anar Mulgoa
Anda
Anderson
Andharyo
Anfas
Anjawain
Anjbin
Anjirya

Anokha Sarda
Anopan
Anora
Anphus
Anupam
Appas
Appayya Shetty
Applepasand
Areca
Arisalumanu
Arka Anmol
Arka Aruna
Arka Neel Kiran
Arka Puneet
Aroumanis
Arthigunda
Aruda
Arumanis (Aroemanis)
Arun
Arundal
Arya Samaj
Aryavartham Irsala
Asa Pillsburry
Asakapalli Baramasi
Asaujia Deoband
Asaujia Surkha
Ashadio
Ashokgaja
Ashruf-us-Samar
Asifpasand
Asojia
Asquith
Assal Kalepad
Assalu Ganneru
Aswina
Athimadhuram
Athizaz Pasand
Aurea
Au-Rumani
Avadh-Ki-Shaam
Aziz Pasand
Azizussamar
Azod Sindurio
Azum-Us-Samar

Babri
Badaigol
Badam
Badam Mamidi
Badam Model
Badashaha
Baderkhandi
Badhanga
Badrul Asmar
Badsha Pasand
Bagal Sarai
Bael Variety
Bagrain
Badhua Baramasi
Bahuddin
Baishakhi
Balakonda
Balaram Bhog
Banana-1
Banarasi Appas
Banarasi Batli
Banchhoda
Bandarubondam
Bangalora
Bangalora Goa
Bangalora Safeda
Banganpalli
Bangaratheegalu
Bangaru Mamidi
Banglawala
Banka
Bannada Kukku
Banshariq
Bansod
Bappakai
Baptiste
Bara Malda
Bara Sinduria
Baramas Dharampur
Baramasia
Baramasi Abra
Baramasi Agaibhagar
Baramasi Ahra
Baramasi Bahua
Baramasi Mahso

Baramasi Malik
Baramasi Pinjor
Bara Rogni
Barashahi
Barbalia
Bardex Musarat
Barmana
Barreto
Bastarda
Bathuie (Bathua)
Batlee
Bauria
Beauty Maclean
Beera
Begam Khas
Began Pasand
Begam Small
Begamphali
Begamphuli
Begum Palli Big
Bekurad
Belgaja
Belkhas
Bellari
Belya
Bem Corada
Benazir
Benazir Amirganj
Benazir Amir Pasand
Benazir Sandilla
Bengali Baramasi
Bengali Gola
Bengali Pairi
Benishan
Benki
Bennet Alphonso
Beria Safdar Pasand
Betasundari
Bettasya
Betti Amba
Bettutukra
Bhabani
Bhadai
Bhadalyan Gola
Bhadauran

Bhadayandaula
Bhadua Lamba
Bhaduri
Bhaduriya
Bhaggunda
Bharat Bhog
Bharat Early
Bharbhuzan
Bhavarapu Irsala
Bhawani Chowras
Bhelua
Bhimalipadva
Bhoordas
Bhopdya
Bhopli
Bhungya
Bhura
Bhurya
Bhutta Irsala
Bhutto
Bhutto Bombay
Bihari Wala
Bijoragarh
Bimli (Bimala)
Binoboy
Birbal
Biru Pasand
Bishop
Bishwanathmukh
Bizcclo
Black Andrews
Black Columban
Blackman
Blanco
Bobbili Chinnakayalu
Bobbili Punasa
Bobri
Boddu Ganneru
Bokkudumanu
Bollo
Bombai
Bombai Abdul Haq
Bombai Kalkafia
Bombai Khirra
Bombay Bhutto

Bombay Black
Bombay Darsha
Bombay Glass
Bombay Great
Bombay Green
Bombay Peda
Bombay Sijid
Bombay Surat
Bombay Yellow
Borbacha
Boribo
Borsha Kalamsar
Bourbon
Brahm-Kai-Mia
Branko Karel
Bride of Russia
Brindabani
Brooks
Bsor
Buddipasand
Buddu Ka Kelwa
Budha
Bulbulchasm
Burhanguti
Buxton Spice

Cacipura
Calabash
Calcutta Amin
Calcutta Baramasi
Calcutta Kharjur
Calcutta Safeda
Calcuttio
Cambodiana
Camoes
Carabao
Caracao de Boi
Cardoz Mankurad
Caribou (Caribao)
Carlotaps
Carreira
Carreira Branca
Carrie
Cecelia Carvelho
Cecil

Celebration
Cereiese
Ceylon
Challenger
Chalta Khas
Chambatan
Champa
Champa Kelwa
Chanamunda
Chandan
Chandbibi
Chandrakaran
Chandrama
Chapti
Chata
Chatrapati
Chatterjeekhas
Chebeliwala
Cheep
Chelukalamanu
Chembu
Cherattapuri Goa
Cherukrasam
Cherumani
Chikarasam
Chikna
Chim Bari
Chimpata
Chinna Kalam
Chinnakothakaya
Chinna Suvarnarekha
Chinnarasam
Chiratpedebaramasi
Chiratputti
Chiripurta
Chitla Afaq
Chitta
Chittoor
Chittoor Puttu
Chittor Badami
Chittor Malgoa
Chittor Rumani
Chor Sindurio
Chota Jehangir
Chuckla
Chudigola

Cidrao
Cluster
Coconut Pasand
Collace
Collaso Branca
Collector
Coloured Chausa
Cooper Green
Cooper Red
Cora
Coracao de Boi
Corozal
Costa
Cowasji Patel
Cream
Creeping
Crimson Blush
Croton
Cushman

Dabba
Dabbila Mamidi
Dabsha
Dabya
Daccai
Dadamiyo
Dadha Peda
Dadoda
Dahiar
Dahipatti
Dalbadal
Dalbia
Dalimbya
Dampera
Darbhanga
Darshan
Dashehra Ambadi
Dattapuri
Davis Haden
Davy's
Dedseri
Delicious
Deorukhio
Derrubada
Devsavali Theya
    Mamidi

Dessert Apple
Devon
Dewn
Dhalna
Dhupa
Dilaram
Dil Bahar
Dil Roson
Dildar
Dilfareb
Dilhouse
Dilkash
Dilkhush
Dilpasand
Dilranjan
Dilsad
Dilwala
Divine
Dixon
Doctor Pasand
Dodi
Dola Bhaduriya
Dom Fernando
Dom Felipe
Donda Kayalumanu
Doodia
Doodia Mulgova
Doodkhirsa
Doodmishri
Doodpeda
Dooma
Dophala
Dophool
Dori
Dos
Dot
Dourada
Doux Doux
Dramayo
Dudhia Gola
Dudhia Hakimuddinpur
Dudho
Dudsho
Dudul
Duncan
Durbate

Durgilal Bhadayan
Durr-e-behist
Durragari Pandhu
Dusheri Aman

Early Florigon
Early Gold
Edward
Elichi
Eldon
Elephand Head
Elivaru Nalla Mamidi
Enayet Pasand
Ennamandala Goa
Ennamandala Theya
    Mamidi
Eruvadi Bangalore
Eruvadi Neelum
Eruvadi Rumani
Espada
Extrema
Ezazusmar

Fairchild
Faizanson
Fajari White
Fajri
Fajri Gola
Fajri Langra Baramasi
Fajri Long
Fajri Zafran
Fakirwala
Fakr-us-Samar
Farhat Afza
Faruhuddin
Fascell
Fazali
Fazali Kalan
Fazali Long
Fazli Malda
Fazli Zumko
Ferdous Pasand
Ferhad
Fernandin
Ferrao
Figureiredo

Filipina
Firangiludva
Florigon
Fonia
Footgola Darbhanga
Fottio
Fragrance
Frias
Fulambary
Furtado

G-8
Gaddemar
Gadgi
Gadoong
Gafarya
Gandevi Selection
    No. 11
Gandevi Selection
    No. 46
Gaurav
Gauri Nishan
Gaurjit
Gendya
George
Ghadyali
Ghoppa
Gibbons
Giddalur Amini
Gilas
Gira Amba
Glenn
Goa
Goa Alphonse
Goa Bunder
Goa Hapus
Goa Mango
Goa Mankur
Goba Sundari
Godabari
Godgo
Godhadya
Gola (Gollah)
Gola Bhadaiyan
Gola Necknoor
Golandas

Golap Bas
Golden Brooks
Golek
Golapalle Sora Mamidi
Gomantaki
Gondoo
Gooli
Gopal Bhog
Gopalapatnam
Gopalkhas
Gopta
Gopta of Navarasi
Gottipalli Baramasi
Gouveia
Govindgarh No.1
Govindgarh No.2
Graham
Grosbeck
Gulab Jaman
Gulab Khas
Gulab Khas Green
Gulab Khas Red
Gulabi
Gulaya
Guldana
Gulkand
Gummadi Ganneru
Gundra Banganapalli
Gundrasam
Gundu
Gurgel
Gurivireddi Pasand
Gurpur
Gurudi
Guruvam

Habib-ul-Samar
Haden
Haden Carabao
Haffez-Be-Gola
Hajipur Langra
Hajkishore
Haldemoni
Haldibas
Hamlet
Handal

Hansraj
Hanuman Bhog
Hanumantha Goa
Hapus Gola
Harabhara
Harbiya
Hardas
Hardil Aziz
Hasara
Hathijhul
Hayati
Hazoor Pasand
Heart
Heer
Heidi
Heinlein
Herman
Hilario
Hilsapeti
Himampasand
Himanshu
Himyat Pasand
Himayuddin
Himsagar
Hindustan Bali
H.L.H.
Hirasonia
Hitlar Pasand
Hood
Htaik-pank
Hur
Husain Fasli
Hushnara
Hussain
Hyder Saheb
Hyderabad
Hyderabad Black
Hyderabad Long
Hyderabad Small

Ilar
Ilsa Peti
Imam Pasand
Imperial
Indonesia
Innanje

Intemax
Irubhogam
Irwin
Israli Mamidi
Itamaraca
Itruiba
Itrulia

Jacquelin
Jaffna
Jafrani
Jagannath Bhog
Jagat Swami
Jagatraman
Jahapasand
Jailor
Jalal Saheb
Jali Bundha
Jalmorni
Jalsain
Jamadar
Jamb
Jami Mamidi
Jampulu
Janab
Janardhan Pasand
Japani Bairainch
Jasmin
Java
Jawahar
Jehanara
Jehangir
Jennifer
Jeronimo
Jhumko Fazli
Jilledikayalu
Jithuvari
Joe Welch
Jogari
Jogia Kakran
Johnson
Jose
Julie

K. Borsha
Kachchaswadi

Kachmuha
Kachura
Kadalia
Kadiri
Kaew
Kailwa Champa
Kailwa Durgilal
Kaithki
Kaitki Bihar
Kaitki Furrukhabad
Kaitki Nizam Ahmad
Kaitki Saiyed Niaz
    Ahmed
Kajal Fazli
Kajali
Kaju
Kakarana Kela
Kakaria (Kakadiya)
Kakaria Amin
Kakaria Jadhra
Kakaria Kalan
Kakaria Stud
Kakran
Kakula Mamidi
Kala
Kala Bansi
Kala Chini
Kala Khoont
Kala Malda
Kalad
Kalagandaras
Kalakand
Kalakanda
Kalam-e-Hindustan
Kalamulgoa
Kalanka Goa
Kalapahar
Kalapani
Kalepad
Kali Bhog
Kalipari
Kalkachi
Kallapady Kovan
Kalmi
Kalua
Kalwaggada

Kamani
Kamochha
Kanai Singh
Kanakanadi
Kancha Mitha
Kancha Swadi
Kanchan
Kanchan Gola
Kanchan Khosal
Kanchanapasand
Kanchankasa
Kandel
Kanka Baniyaz Ahmad
Kantulu Mamidi
Kapatabhanga
Kapri
Karania
Karanjio
Karaspet
Kare-Ka-Fazli
Kare-Many
Karel
Karela Bhagalpur
Karelia
Karpuram
Karpurkeli
Karuind
Karutha Kolamban
Kasi Ratnalu
Kasturi
Kasturi Mamidi
Katarya
Katiki Syed Niaz
    Ahmad
Kayo Savoy
Keitt
Kela
Kelya (Bonardi)
Kelya (Menawali)
Kelya (Nandgaon)
Kelya No.2 (Menavali)
Kemsagar
Kensington
Kent
Keo Saaht
Kesar

Kesar Basti
Khajar
Khajia
Khandeshi
Khangari Bacha
Khanum Pasand
Khara Malda
Kharbuja
Kharjur
Kharki
Khasa Ibrahimpur
Khasulkhas
Khasulkhas Shahabad
Khatashi
Khatima
Khatimul Khair
Khatta Gola
Kheera
Khirpuri
Khirsapat
Khobarya
Khobarya (Big)
Khodi
Khoja
Khudadad
Khudadad Long
Khuddus
Kidang
Kijosawy
Kilimook
Kimaji
Kini
Kintalvanipeta
Kir Tatti
Kirania
Kishen Bhog
Kitovu
Kodur Chinnarasam
Kodur Goa
Kodur Selection
Kogettira
Kohinoor
Kohitoor
Koikalbian
Kolanka Gova
Kondiah Mamidi

Korakam
Koral
Koram Goa
Kota Manga
Kothapalli Chinna
    Arisalu
Kothapalli Kobbari
Kothi Hyderabad
Kowthar
Krishnaraopasand
Kristaphal
Kshira Sindhu
Kuanpaharia
Kudethoor
Kudurekukku
Kulas
Kumarpahar
Kumra Jali
Kumwenda
Kunchan Mitha
Kurashige
Kurhadya
Kurkan
Kurnulu Malgoa

Ladankoo
Ladavio
Laddu
Lahsun
Laila
Lajawab Malihabad
Lajat Bahsh
Lakhna (Malda)
Lal Bhadainya
Lal Khatra
Lal Mulgoa
Lal Muni
Lal Pairi
Lal Sundari
Lalji
Langra
Langra Banaras
Langra Bengal
Langra Calcutta
Langra Digha
Langra Dudhia

Langra Gorakhpur
Langra Hajipur
Langra Large
Langry Lyallpur
Langra Rampur
Langra Sabour
Largo
Larshkarshikan
Lata
Lata Bombay
Latchayyapeta
Lateef Aliwalla
Latif-us-Samar
Latkampoo
Latra
Layra
Lazzat Baksh
Ledignda
Lemon
Lilao
Lippens
Litchi
Local
Loha Chur
Lohra
Long Green
Lord
Lotan
Love-e-Mosgul
Lucio-I
Lungagndi
Luzonmang

M-13269
Mabroka
Maca Apple
Machli
Machmanlie
Madame Frances
Madame Macpherson
Madan-Ban
Madhavaraopasand
Madhukuppi
Madhulika
Madras
Madarasi Aphoos

Madu
Magovar
Magshimim
Mahalanjio
Maharaj Pasand
Maharaj Pasand Kafoori
Maharaja of Mysore
Maharajah
Maharani
Mahiparia (Acharwala)
Mahmooda Vikarbad
Mahmud Bahar
Mahmuda
Mahmudulsamar
Mahorajpasand
Mahu
Majanu
Majjvalasa Veesamenu
Makaram
Makhsoor
Malai
Malai Mishri
Malcovda
Malda
Malda Bombay Green
Malda Gola
Malda Handle
Maldahe
Maldej
Malgessa
Malinh
Mallavva Mamidi
Mallick Wonder
Mallihabadi
Mallika
Mallipandri Gulabi
Manda
Mandhoppa
Mandi
Mandi Khangarti
Mandi Khil
Mandragi
Manga
Mangla Veelario
Mango Bhuradas
Mangolar

Mangotina Type
Manjira
Mankurad
Manohar
Manoranjan
Manoratha
Manthota Bahuddin
Manzanillo Nujnez
Manzano
Marina
Markeara
Martinique
Masana
Matetin
Mateus
Maya
Meenakshi
Menaka
Mettavalasa
    Pecchumanu
Mewa Fajri
Miltana Sundershah
Mirio
Mirzafar
Mishri Bhog
Mishri Dana
Mishrikand
Miss Harwood
Mithawa Bihar
Mithe
Mithuwa
Mithuwa Ghazipur
Mithuwa Malda
Mithuwa Sunder Red
Mittari
Modya
Mogarya
Mohamadwala
Mohan Thakur
Mohanbhog
Mohsin
Mokka Banganpalli
Mokka Collector
Mokka Gulabi
Mokkuvva
Mombasa

Momi-K
Monarein
Monserrate de Bardez
Monserrate de Salcette
Monserrate White
Moolki No.1
Moovandan
Moreh
Motichur
Mouse
Muffarai
Mukku Ganneru
Mukku Goa
Mukkurasam
Mukri
Mulgoa
Mulgoa Black
Mulgoa Black Long
Mulgoa Black Round
Mulgoa Deshi
Mulgoa Kasturi
Mulgoa Lal
Mulgoa Roogan
Mumbaigaro
Munda Phata (in Orissa)
Mundappa (in Tamal
    Nadu)
Mundappa Black
Mundappa White
Murshidabad
Musharad Sashti
Musharat Bardesh
Musherad Safet
Musherad Tambada
Mushrad
Muthuwar Pasand
Muvandan Black
Muvandan White
Mylapuri
Mylelpelian

Nabdar
Nadan
Nadasala
Nadiagaja
Nagasagaram

Nagau
Nagin
Nagulapalli Irsala
Nagya
Nakka
Nakkalampeddamamidi
Nakli Bombay
Naliyaro
Nalla Andrews
Nalla Mamidi
Nalla Rasam
Nam-doc-mai
Namtal
Nandanam
    Peddamamidi
Nangilleri
Naomi
Narayanarajupadva
Narela
Narela Andrews
Nargis
Nari Keli
Narikel Thaki
Naseem Pasand
Nasik Pasand
Naspati
Nasrat Pasand
Nastota
Nathu Mulgoa
Nati Husenamma
    Pasand
Naudha
Naudha Inayat Khan
Naudha Miyan Saheb
Nauras
Nauratna
Navabasamadi
Navaneetham
Nawab
Nawab Mamidi
Nawab Pasand
Nayan Bhog
Nazeem Pasand
Neelai Pasand
Neeleshan Gujarat
Neeleshwari

Neelgoa
Neelum Madrasi
Neelosari
Neelphanso
Neeluddin
Neelum
Neelum II
Nekkare
Neldica
Neldwan
Neliero
Nelukrit
Nelva Ganneru
Nemlikantam
Nettayam
Ngowe
Nicolan Afonsa
Nimrod
Niranjan
Nisar Pasand
Non-Plus-Untra
Noonam
Noonepasand
Nurjehan
Nuwan Chan
Nuzurd Theya Mamidi
Nuzwid Pedda Mamidi
Nyattikuzian

Octonumber Mulgoa
Okrong
Oliveira-Neto
Olour
Ono
Osteen
Owbak

P.S. Special No.1
P.S. Special No.2
P.S. Special No.3
P.S. Special No.4
Pacharasi
Padiri
Padmanabha Goa
Parharpur Sinduria
Paheri

Pahilwan
Pahutan
Paiposha
Pairi
Pairi Bengali
Pairi Irani
Pairi Kanara
Pairi Poona
Pairi Sindhi
Paispasand
Pajara
Palmer
Palura
Panaji
Panakalu
Panchadarakalasa
Panchadarlamanu
Panchavarnam
Pandharpurya
Panja Pasand
Pansera
Papaya
Papaya Khas
Papayyaraju Goa
Papel
Papel Branco
Paria Selection
Parnad
Parrot
Parsapalli Dodia
Parsi Shrivanco
Pasand
Pathre
Pau
Paushia
Payposha
Peach
Pear
Pearafulli
Pedda Ganneru
Pedda Khader
Pedda Neelum
Pedda Rasam
Pedda Suvarnarekha
Peddakalepadu
Perelouis

Peres
Peta Sweet
Peta Theya Mamidi
Peter
Pethol
Phokraj
Pico
Pina Type
Pinnivemali Baramasi
Pirankoela
Pirthi
PKM-1
Pochhatio
Podugu Banganpalli
Pol-amba
Polgola Dharbhanga
Police
Polyembryo
Popat Piari
Popatia
Porkal
Potalma
Pote
Prabhasankar
Primor de Amoreira
Prince
Prior
Pukhraj
Pulihora
Purainia
Puri
Puroshottam Bhog
Puthi
Puttu

Radhika Bhog
Ragushantaki
Rahim Pasand
Rahri
Rai Bhog
Raj Lotan
Raj Rani
Raja Pasand
Raja Ram Puri
Rajabadai
Rajabahadur

Rajabhog
Rajabunder
Rajapuri
Rajawala
Rajiv
Rajmam
Rajuganneru
Rajumanu
Ralimay
Ram Kela
Ram Pasand
Ram Prasad
Rambhog
Ramphalva
Rana
Ranee Pasand
Ranee's White
Rangar
Rangoon Goa
Rangroji
Ranitella Kayalu
Rao Shah
Rari
Rasabale
Rasalrot
Rasgola
Rashk-e-Galistan
Rashk-e-Jahan
Raspoonia
Raspunia
Raspuri
Rataul
Ratna
Rawanya
Reario
Rebel
Reddi
Reddi Pasand
Redondo
Redsi
Regular
Regunta Sora Mamidi
Rehman Khas
Rehman Pasand
Reinol
Remedios

Rogni
Rohir Murho
Romani
Romanio
Rooh-e-Jhan
Roos
Root Jack
Rosa
Roshan Tepak
Rote
Royal Special
Ruby
Rumani
Rupee
Ruzwani

Sabia
Sabja
Sabre
Sabri
Sabsang
Sabzdaraj
Sacretina
Sadaat
Sadabahar
Sadaphal
Sadawala
Safaida
Safar Pasand
Safed Amini
Safed Mulgoa
Safeda Calcutta
Safeda Gola
Safeda Jawahar
Safeda Lucknow
Safeda Malihabad
Safeda Sharbati Kalai
Safeda Sherbati
Sagarlangra
Sahajan
Saigon
Sakhar-Gooty
Sakkar China
Sakkar Gutli
Sakkarpara
Salappa

Salarsummer
Salebhoy Amidi
Salem
Salem Badam
Salem Bangalora
Salgada
Salgadinha
Salim
Sam-Ru-Du
Samar Bahist Alibagh
Samar Bahist Rampur
Samar-e-Behist
Samarbehist Chowsa
Samarkand
Samini
Sampee
Sanapatia
Sandersha
Sangtra
Sanna-Veli-Mav
Sannakalu
Sans Pareille
Santa Alexandrina
Santana
Santiago
Saraum
Sarbati Brown
Sarda
Sardar
Sardar Pasnad
Sared Mulgoa
Sarghoda
Sarikha
Sarkar Kilimuk
Saru
Sasmbandan
Satir Kara
Saugandhia
Saunfia
Saurabh
Savera
Schobank
Sebe Hind
Secretina
Seetabhog
Seethaphal Gola

Sehroli
Senora
Sensation
Sepia
Sepia Shah Pasand
Seri
Seri Khas
Serikaya
Ses
Seven-in-one
Shadulla
Shadwala
Shagapu Goa
Shah Behati
Shah Pasnad
Shahbela
Shahir
Shahjehan
Shakarkand (Dhakla)
Shakarkand (Thorla)
Shaker Gola
Shamsul-Asamar
Sharbati Begrain
Sharbati Brown
Sharbati Gadi
Shareritmaon
Sharifa
Sheill
Shelly
Shendadya
Shendriya
Shepya
Sherbatanar
Shervanio
Shesh Mari
Shibata
Shiraj Pasand
Shiredachan
Shivaji Pasand
Shori
Shova Pasand
Shravan Dodi
Shurmai Fazli
Shurola
Shyam Sundar
Sidrali

Silapua
Simmonds
Sin Chitla
Sinbaung
Sindhri
Sindhu
Sindhura
Singapuri
Singharha
Singra
Sipia Shah Pasand
Sirohi
Siroli
Siruvel Jehangir
Sita Bhog
Sitaphal
Smith
Sobewali Ting
Sobpasand
Sohan Halwa
Sona Tol
Sonada (Narsingh Bhog)
Sonar
Soramamidi
Soridhan
Sorikhas
Sorkamathi
Soundadya
Soya Kalan
Springfels
Starch
Strothman
Subhash
Sugar King
Sukh Tara
Sukharia
Sukul
Sukul Clinia
Sultan Buzurg
Sultan Pasand
Sultan-us-Samar
Sundar Pasnad
Sundari
Sundarimath
Sunderja
Sunder Langra

Sunderprasad
Sundersha Hyderabad
Sundersha Kumta
Sundry
Sunhari
Sunneri
Sunset
Surababu
Surangudi
Surja Puri
Surkh Burma
Surkha
Surkha Abdul Aziz
Surkha Baramasi
Surkha Calcutta
Surkha Chaudhary
Surkha Dr. Pasand
Surkha Kudratulla
Surkha Mohinuddinpur
Surkha Panditwala
Surkha Sida Faruq
Surkha Sikari
Surki
Surma Fazli
Surmandani
Suvarnarekha
Swanen
Swantham
Swaranlata
Swarapadu
Swarna Jehangir
Sweet

Tahar
Taimur Pasand
Taimurlang
Taimurya
Talapet
Tamancha
Tana
Tango
Tangue
Tansera
Tardalu
Tata Amadi
Tazumeik

Tehri
Tella Gulabi
Temuda
Tenneru
Tephala
Thabelu
Thagarampudi Theya
    Mamidi
Thambra
Thankingamadi
Tharipadi
Thaviti Goa
Theega
Theki
Thella Ayodhya
Thella Gulabi
Thelukalumanu
Theya Banganapalli
Thimmapuram
    Doravukattu Theya
    Mamidi
Thorang
Thou-lou-to-daung
Thripurasundari
Thurri
Thurum
Tikia Farash
Tilka Bhadainya
Timod
Timun
Tofa
Tofancha
Tolbert
Tommy Atkins
Tong-dum
Topisundari
Toranja
Totafareed
Totafari
Totapari
Totapari Green
Totapari Hyderabad
Totapuri Kumta
Totapuri Ratnagiri
Totapari Red Small
Totapuri Small Red

Trotum
Tunikalu
Turpentine
Tyler Premier

Udage
Udyan Sundari
Ulliar
Undulli
Unnabi Gola

Valoti Dadamio
Van Dyke
Van Raj
Vanka Neelum
Varun
Vashi Badami
Vatganga
Vattam
Vazeer Pasand
Velia Gola
Velia Kota Manga
Velio

Vellai Kolumban
Vellakachi
Verpanas
Viceroy
Vijai Raogarh
Vimond
Vishwanath Mukh
Vulua

Waden
Walat Pasnad
Walkya
Wallahahpasand
Wallajah
Washi Badan
Willard
Wiliam Saheb

Xavier

Yakut Rumani
Yakuti
Yekkar

Yellamandala
    Thiyyamamidi
Yerra Gulabi
Yerra Mamidi
Yerra Mulgoa
Yerrakayalu Baramasi
Yerukunaidu Baramasi

Zafar Ali
Zafarani Gola
Zafarani Shahabad
Zafari
Zafran
Zali Bhang
Zamurad
Zarda
Zardalu
Zardamin
Zawnia
Zilete (Zillate)
Zill
Zumistania

Appendix 3

WHERE TO FIND 'EM, HOW TO GET 'EM

Nurseries, Garden Clubs, and Festivals

NURSERIES

For those of us who grow mangoes in our own backyards, no store-brought fruit can equal the taste of the homegrown variety. Mangoes are hardy plants, and you don't need a green thumb to grow them. For those who have small backyards or mere patios, the Cogshall and Julie varieties, both dwarfs, are prolific producers. For those of you with a bit more space to work with, the sky's the limit.

Probably the best place in America to buy trees is at Fairchild Tropical Gardens' Annual International Mango Festival, held in early July in Miami. The 2000 festival featured twelve hundred trees for sale, representing twenty-one varieties. And the price was right: $15 each for sturdy three-footers. That's the good part. The bad part is you had to cool your heels in a line of people that snaked around the building, and the 2000 crop was sold out in fifteen minutes.

ARIZONA

Phoenix's Tropica Mango Nursery offers ten varieties of mangoes and more for tropical fruit fanciers. Contact Tropica Mango Nursery, 3015 E. Baseline Road, Phoenix, AZ 85040. Phone: (888) 942-6577.

AUSTRALIA

Birdwood Nursery in Queensland specializes in fruit trees and has mango trees available. Contact Birdwood Nursery, 71-83 Blackall Range Road, Nambour, Queensland, Australia 4560. Phone: (07) 5442 1611; fax: (07) 5442-1053; e-mail: birdwood1@optusnet.com.au.

CALIFORNIA

J. D. Andersen Nursery offers Asian and Indian variety mangoes along with the popular California variety, Edgehill. Nursery address: 2790 Marvinga Lane, Fallbrook, CA 92028. Phone: (760) 723-2907. Contact the company's offices at J. D. Andersen Nursery, 2961 Calle Frontera, San Clemente, CA 92673. Phone (949) 361-3652; fax: (949) 492-2198. The website is www.jdandersen.com.

California Tropical Fruit Tree Nursery carries a wide selection of mango trees, including the Edward, Glenn, Haden, Kent, Manila, Okrung, Pim Saen Mun, Tommy Atkins, and Valencia Pride varieties. The nursery is located in Vista; the company's offices are in Carlsbad. Contact California Tropical Fruit Tree Sales, 580 Beech Avenue, Suite A., Carlsbad, CA 92008. Phone: (760) 434-5085; fax: (760) 434-1460. The nursery is open Monday through Saturday from 9 A.M. to 5 P.M. and Sunday from 9 A.M. to 1 P.M.

Pacific Tree Farms carries a wide variety of trees, including the California variety, Edgehill. Others in stock include Bombay, Carrie, Chuchua, Edward, Glenn, Haden, Jakarta, Julie, Keitt, Kent, Nam Doc Mai, and Oro. Contact Pacific Tree Farms, 4301 Lynwood Drive, Chula Vista, CA 91910-3226. Phone: (619) 422-2400.

FLORIDA

Alan Smith specializes in multigrafted trees for mango-lovers cursed with limited yard space. He'll also do custom grafts for you if time permits. His nursery offers Florida varieties plus Caribbean special Buxton Spice and Jakarta varieties. Call ahead for an appointment before your visit. Contact Alan Smith Tropical Fruit Trees, 7341 121st Terrace North, Largo, FL 33773. Phone: (727) 539-7527; fax: (727) 536-9342; e-mail: zambesi@gte.net.

Blind Hog Groves provides mangoes for the southwestern portion of the state. Contact Blind Hog Groves, 6355 Pineland Road, P.O. Box 408, Pineland, FL 33945. Phone: (941) 283-4092; fax: (941) 283-3175.

Brookstone's Wonderland provides trees for fanciers in northern Miami-Dade County. Contact Brookstone's Wonderland, 17401 NW 19th Avenue, Opa-Locka, FL 33056. Phone: (305) 625-0921.

Drive south to the Redlands and nearby areas of southwestern Miami-Dade County for variety in mangoes. Here are a few nurseries to try.

David's Garden Nursery
3900 S.W. 99th Avenue
Miami, FL 33165
Phone: (305) 382-0339

Grapeland Nursery
16701 S.W. 200th Street
Miami, FL 33187
Phone: (305) 252-8524

Lara Farms Nursery
18660 S.W. 200th Street
Miami, FL 33187
Phone: (305) 253-2750

Pine Island Nursery
16300 S.W. 184 Street
Miami, FL 33187
Phone: (305) 233-5501
Fax: (305) 233-5610
E-mail: glowalt@earthlink.net

Ray's Nursery of Miami
18905 S.W. 177th Avenue
Miami, FL 33177
Phone: (305) 255-3589

Garden of Delights is an exotic fruit mail-order nursery in Broward County that sells mangoes of the Julie, Carrie, and Okrung varieties. Contact Garden of Delights, 14560 S.W. 14th Street, Davie, FL 33325-4217. Phone: (800) 741-3103; fax: (954) 236-4588.

Zill High Performance Plants provides outstanding mango plants for the wholesale market. South Florida Home Depot stores carry them, and the Palm Beach Rare Fruit Council's sales feature them as well. Contact Zill High Performance Plants, 6801 107th Place, Boynton Beach, FL 33437. Phone: (561) 732-355; fax: (561) 364-4884.

Jose Puras sells seeds for Toledo mangoes over the Internet from his home in Palm Bay in Brevard County. Contact him at www.caribbeanseeds.com.

HAWAII

Imamura Nursery is located on the Big Island of Hawaii. Contact Imamura Nursery, 14 Hiluhilu Street, Hilo, HI 96730. Phone: (808) 959-9570.

ISRAEL

Haskelberg Nursery sells plants of the Maya, Tommy Atkins, Kent, and Keitt varieties on three types of rootstock. Contact Haskelberg Nursery, Kfar Vitkin 40200, Israel. Phone: 972-9-8666384; fax: 972-50-377775. The website is www.persimmon.co.il.

GARDEN CLUBS

To expand your knowledge of mangoes and learn how to select and care for them, the many horticultural gardens and garden clubs provide a wealth of information for mango lovers, from novices to mavens. Here are some great places to turn.

CALIFORNIA

California Rare Fruit Growers, Inc.
5081 Dartmouth Avenue
Westminster, CA 92683

Established in 1968, CRFG is the world's largest amateur fruit-growing organization, with members in nearly every U.S. state and thirty countries. Local councils are in areas throughout the state including the Central Coast, Central Valley, Foothills, Golden Gate, Inland Empire, Los Angeles, Monterey Bay, Northern San Diego County, Orange County, Redwood Empire, Sacramento Valley, San Diego, Santa Clara Valley, South San Joaquin Valley, South Bay, Ventura/Santa Barbara, and West Los Angeles, and in the Houston, Texas, and Mesa, Arizona, areas. Benefits of membership include a seed bank, *The Fruit Gardener Magazine* and a variety of publications, an annual fruit festival, and more. CRFG operates a great website (www.crfg.org) and online resources.

FLORIDA

Brevard Rare Fruit Council
P.O. Box 3773
Indialantic, FL 32903

Plant fanciers on Florida's Space Coast are well served by the **Brevard Rare Fruit Council**, which boasts members from around the state. The club's excellent newsletter is available online at www.brevardrarefruit.org. Meetings are on the fourth Wednesday of every month at Melbourne's Front Street Civic Center except November and December. The November meeting is usually a banquet on the Wednesday of the week before Thanksgiving. There is no December meeting.

Broward County Rare Fruit and Vegetable Council
Broward County Cooperative Extension Service
3245 College Avenue
Davie, FL 33314
Phone: (954) 370-3725

The council meets at 7:30 P.M. on the first Monday of every month.

Caloosa Rare Fruit Exchange
Lee County Extension Office
Terry Park
3406 Palm Beach Boulevard
Ft. Myers, FL 33916

This is one of Florida's most active rare fruit councils. The group publishes a cookbook, maintains a tree bank, and also presents an annual tropical fruit festival. Meetings are held on the first Tuesday of every month at 7:30 P.M.

Fairchild Tropical Garden
10901 Old Cutler Road
Miami, FL 33156
Phone: (305) 667-1651
Fax: (305) 661-8953
Website: www.ftg.org

Surely, the eighty-three-acre Fairchild Tropical Garden, established in 1938 by botanist David Fairchild, is Miami-Dade County's Garden of Earthly Delights. For mango lovers, the International Mango Festival is the ultimate weekend activity (see Chapter 3). The park is open from 9:30 A.M. to 4:30 P.M. every day except Christmas.

Fruit and Spice Park
24801 S.W. 187th Avenue
Homestead, FL 33031
Phone: (305) 247-5727
Fax: (305) 245-3369

Owned by the Metro-Dade Parks and Recreation Department, this thirty-acre public park is the only facility of its type in the United States. More than five hundred tropical and exotic varieties of fruits, vegetables, spices, nuts, herbs, and other plants of note grow there. Established in 1944 in the Redlands farming area of southwestern Miami-Dade County, the park is a bit of a drive for many people but well worth the effort. One highlight is the Mangoes, Mangoes, Mangoes workshop in late June. Other programs are also of interest to mango lovers. The park is open from 10 A.M. to 5 P.M. daily except Thanksgiving, Christmas, and New Year's Day.

Manatee Rare Fruit Council
P.O. Box 1656
Bradenton, FL 34206
Phone: (941) 729-5985

The council meets the second Monday of every month at 7 P.M. at the Harlee Auditorium in Palmetto. Among the annual events is a tropical tree sale featuring mangoes.

Mounts Botanical Gardens
531 North Military Trail
West Palm Beach, FL 33401
Phone: (561) 968-7194

A mere fourteen acres, but what a place! The annual tropical plant extravaganza features a wide variety of mango cultivars for sniffing and sampling. Open Monday through Saturday from 8:30 A.M. to 4:30 P.M. and Sundays from 1 P.M. to 5 P.M.

Palm Beach Chapter, Rare Fruit Council International
P.O. Box 16464
Palm Beach, FL 33416-6464
Phone: (561) 791-2837
Fax: (561) 641-3028

Among the chapter's many activities are plant sales featuring mangoes and an August ice cream party featuring exotic fruit flavors. The council meets at 7:30 P.M. on the second Friday of every month at Mounts Botanical Gardens Auditorium, 531 North Military Trail, West Palm Beach. Phone: (561) 968-7194.

Sarasota Fruit and Nut Society
P.O. Box 536
Nokomis, FL 34274
Phone: (941) 966-4377
E-mail: Crux@gte.net

Meetings for the group are on the second Wednesday of every month at 6:45 P.M. at the Edison Keith Mansion at Phillippi Creek Park, 5500 South Tamiami Trail, Sarasota. One of the club's annual highlights is a rare tropical fruit tree sale.

FESTIVALS

During Florida's torrid summers, why would you possibly want to get hotter cooking over a hot stove when you could be sipping a tall, frothy iced mango drink or sampling a delicious mango salad, kabob, or stir-fry prepared by someone else? How about traveling to one of the many mango festivals offered around the globe (if you have some frequent-flyer miles burning a hole in your briefcase) or around south Florida (if you prefer to stay close to home)?

Mutchilba's Mango Mardi Gras, Dimbulah, Queensland, Australia (January)

Mango Mela, Bangalore, India (late May to late June): An annual celebration to boost tourism and promote mango sales, the Mango Mela includes a variety of mango-related activities including a painting competition,

quizzes on mango lore, tastings, and a variety of other cultural activities.

Philippine National Mango Congress, Cebu, Philippines (June)

MangoMania, Pine Island, Florida (June): Held since 1995, MangoMania mixes good sounds, good cheer, and great mangoes on Florida's Left Coast.

Deerfield Beach Mango Festival, Deerfield Beach, Florida (late June or early July): This summer street festival showcases mangoes and many other great tastes of southeast Florida.

Tropical Fruit Fiesta, Key West, Florida (late June or early July): Begun in 1999, this festival features displays, tastings, and tropical fruit experts on hand to teach more about favorite cultivars. Call (305) 292-4501.

Mango Festival, Carmen, Augusan del Norte, Philippines (early July)

International Mango Festival, Fairchild Tropical Gardens, Miami, Florida (July): This weekend festival of mangoes includes tastings, a mango-centric culinary showcase, trees for sale, workshops, and much more. Don't eat before you go; your taste buds will thank you.

International Mango Festival, Talkatora Indoor Stadium, New Delhi, India (July): Begun in 1988 and sponsored by the Delhi Tourism and Transportation Development Corporation, this is the granddaddy of all mango festivals. The three-day event features mango tree sales and tasting opportunities for more than five hundred varieties of mango. In 1998, other mango-growing nations were represented, included Mexico, Pakistan, and Brazil. Exhibits of multi-variety grafted trees are a popular feature; the 1999 festival featured one grafted from more than three hundred varieties. Information stations dispense growing tips and other topics of interest to growers. The festival also has a fun side, with mango folk songs, games, quizzes and puzzles, a mango-eating competition, and a juried mango cooking contest.

Mango Bash, Davie, Florida (July)

Mango Mania, Pinecrest, Florida (throughout July): This festival was begun in 1999 in the Miami-area community.

Northwood Hills Mango Festival, West Palm Beach, Florida (mid to late July): Here's another festival inaugurated in 1999. It's part block party, part bazaar, and part culinary festival, with many cooking contests, fruit for sale, and other fun events.

Ka'u Mango and Music Festival, Pahala (Big Island), Hawaii (late July): This event, at the Pahala Community Center, is as much a cultural exposition as a mango festival. Originated to honor and celebrate the grove of fifty trees in the Old Japanese Mill Camp, the festival is a whirl of good sounds, good vibes, and great food. From mango art to mango tarts, this festival has it all.

Naples Mango Festival, Golden Gate Community Center, Naples, Florida (late July): The 1999 festival was the first, and it was a smash. More than sixty cultivars were on display, along with a variety of mango treats, from the expected (jams, chutneys, and drinks) to the totally unexpected (mango pizza).

Mango Utsav, Chandigarh, India (late July to early August)

Tropical FruitFest, Boca Raton, Florida (early August): Tastings, recipes, and sales of mango and other exotic fruit trees are among the fare at this fair in southeastern Palm Beach County.

Mindanao Mango Congress, Zamboanga City, Philippines (November): Organized by a coalition of mango growers in 1996, this is more an industry convention than a festival.

International Mango Symposium, Pattaya, Thailand (annual): Begun in 1992, the symposium is aimed more at academics studying mango-growing technology and technique than mango fanciers and other party animals. The three-day symposium is sponsored by Kasetsart University and the International Society for Horticultural Science. Delegates come from throughout Thailand and other mango-growing nations.

Selected Bibliography

1894 Transactions of the Queensland Acclimatisation Society. Petrie's Bight, Brisbane, Australia: Pole, Outridge & Co., 1894.

Alexander, D. McE. *The Mango in Australia.* Australia: Commonwealth Scientific and Industrial Research Organization, 1987.

Alexander, D. McE., P. B. Scholefield, and A. Frodsham. *Some Tree Fruits for Tropical Australia.* Australia: Commonwealth Scientific and Industrial Research Organization, 1983.

Amazing Thai Mango. Bangkok: Horticulture Research Institute, Thailand Department of Agriculture, 1999.

Auckland, J. "Mango." Newafrica.com.

Bally, Ian. "Mango Growing in Israel." *Mango Care* (Queensland Department of Primary Industries), No. 19.

Beddoe, T. W. "Mango Varieties in the West Indies." Proceedings of a workshop on the integrated development of mango enterprises in the Caribbean, Trinidad, and Tobago, 1994.

Campbell, Richard J., ed.. *A Guide to Mangos in Florida.* Miami: Fairchild Tropical Gardens, 1992.

Chandler, William Henry. *Evergreen Orchards* Second Edition. Philadelphia: Lea & Febiger, 1958.

Chia, C. L., R. A. Hamilton, and D. O. Evans. "Mango." Commodity Fact Sheet #Man—3(A), Hawaii Cooperative Extension Service, Hawaii Institute of Tropical Agriculture and Human Resources, University of Hawaii at Manoa, July 1988.

Choudhry, Muhammad Aslam, Muhammad Siddique Javel, and Saeed Akbar Zahid. "Export Potential of Mango from Pakistan." *Economic Review,* 27:7 (July 1996): 21, 23.

Crane, J. H., and C. W. Campbell. "The Mango." University of Florida Cooperative Extension Service Fact Sheet #FC-2 (April 1995).

Cunningham, Anthony B. "Ecological Footprint of the Wooden Rhino: Depletion of Hardwoods for the Carving Trade in Kenya." People and Plants Online (www.kew.org.uk/peopleplants/ lessons /case1/html).

Devi, K. S. Usha. "Sweet on the Versatile Mango." *The* (Malaysia) *Star Online* (Cyber Kuali) (1998).

Dhandar, D. G., P. A. Mathew, and S. Subramanian, eds. *Mangoes of Goan Origin with Propagation and Culture.* ICAR Research Complex for Goa (India), Technical Bulletin No. 1 (1997).

"Did you know?" *The* (Kingston) *Daily Gleaner.* (November 24, 1958).

Douthett, Daniel G. "The Mango: Asia's King of Fruits." *Ethnobotanical Leaflets,* Southern Illinois Herbarium.

Du Pavillion, France. *Les Manguiers à L'île Maurice et à L'île Bourbon* Second Edition. Les Salines, Mauritius: Pyrouman Publications/Caslon Printing, 1991.

"E. Java's Mango Export Decreases." *Surabaya Post* (online edition) (July 6, 1997).

Evans, David. "Focus—EU's 25-Year Battle Over Chocolate Ended." Reuters (March 15, 2000).

Fong, Chin Hoong, and Yong Hoi-Sen. *Malaysian Fruits in Colour.* Kuala Lumpur, Malaysia: Tropical Press, SDN. BHD, 1982.

Gangolly, S. R., Ranjit Singh, S. L. Katyal, and Daljit Singh. *The Mango.* New Delhi: Indian Council of Agricultural Research, c. 1957.

Hamilton, R. A., C. L. Chia, and D. O. Evans. "Mango Cultivars in Hawaii." Information Text Series 042-04, College of Tropical Agriculture and Human Resources, University of Hawaii at Manoa, March 1992.

Hau, Vu Cong. *Fruit-Trees in Vietnam.* Hanoi: The Gioi Publishers, 1997.

Herzon, Karen. "Mango Fandango." *Milwaukee Journal Sentinel* (online edition) (June 9, 1999).

Hill, Terry, and David Parr. "Harvesting and Packing Mangoes for Export to Southeast Asia." *Farmnote* (online), f07493.HTM, Agriculture Western Australia (March 11, 1998).

"History of the Mango—How It Came to Jamaica." *The* (Kingston) *Sunday Gleaner* (July 21, 1957).

Holmes, Rowland. "Attendance at the 4th International Mango Symposium, Miami." Report published by the Horticultural Research and Development Corporation, Gordon, Australia, 1997.

Johnson, P. R., and D. Parr. *Mango Growing in Western Australia.* Bulletin 4348, Agdex 234/01, Agriculture Western Australia.

Johnson, Peter. "Mango Developments in China." *Mango Care* (Queensland Department of Primary Industries, Australia), No. 24 (1998): 10–13.

Johnson, Peter. "Mangoes in China." *Mango Care* (Queensland Department of Primary Industries, Australia), No. 23 (1998): 10–13.

"Juicy Times for Citizens as Mango Prices Crash." (Bombay) *Indian Express* (online edition) (June 3, 1999).

Kimhi, M., and I. Kosto. "A Guideline for Mango Production in the Caribbean." Second Regional Workshop on Tropical Fruits: 59–61.

Kolanad, Gitanjali. *Culture Shock! India.* Portland, Oregon: Graphic Arts Center Publishing Co., 1994.

Lynch, S. John, and Margaret J. Mustard. *Mangos in Florida.* Tallahassee: Florida Department of Agriculture.

Mangga: Research, Development, Extension Agenda for Mango. Philippine National Program on Mango Research, Development, and Extension. San Miguel, Jordan, Guimaras, Philippines, 1999.

"Mango." PCARRD (Philippine Council for Agriculture, Forestry, and Natural Resources Research and Development) Online commodity information sheet, 1998.

"Mango Chief, Musveni Okay." *The* (Kampala, Uganda) *Monitor* (online edition) (June 4, 1999).

"Mango-Mania at New Delhi Festival." CNN.com, July 13, 1998.

"Mangoes in Brazil." *Mango Care* (Queensland Department of Primary Industries, Australia), No.26 (November 1998): 14–16.

"Mangoes, the Real Fruit of India!" *Desh-Videsh*, Vol. 3, No. 4 (1997): 34.

Marcus, George, and Nancy Marcus. *Forbidden Fruits and Forgotten Vegetables*. New York: St. Martin's Press, 1982.

Morton, Julia F. *Fruits of Warm Climates*. Miami: Julia F. Morton, 1987

Morton, Kendal, and Julia Morton. *Fifty Tropical Fruits of Nassau*. Coral Gables, Florida: Text House, Inc., 1946.

Mukherjee, S. K. "Origin of Mango *(Mangifera indica)*." *Economic Botany*, Vol. 26 (1972): 260–264.

Munibari, Mahassen Ali, and Amin Alhakimi. "Current State of Horticultural Research in Yemen" Reports from the World Conference on Horticultural Research at Rome, Italy, June 17–20, 1998.

Nair, P. Thankappan. *The Mango in Indian Life and Culture* Part I. Dehra Dun, India: Bishen Singh Mahendra Pal Singh, 1996.

Nair, P. Thankappan. *The Mango in Indian Life and Culture* Part II. Dehra Dun, India: Bishen Singh Mahendra Pal Singh, 1995.

Nazri, M. M. "Cultivation and Utilization of Mango in the Sultanate of Oman." *Economic Review*, 22:22 (July 1991): 23.

"New Taste Sensations." *Mango Care* (Queensland Department of Primary Industries, Australia), No. 29 (January 2000): 2–3.

Payne, Selma, and W. J. A. Payne. *Cooking with Exotic Fruit*. London: B. T. Batsford, 1979.

Pohronezny, Ken, and R. B. Marlatt. "Some Common Diseases of Mango in Florida." Plant Pathology Fact Sheet PP-23, University of Florida Institute of Food and Agricultural Sciences, Florida Cooperative Extension Services, 1993.

Popenoe, Wilson. *Manual of Tropical and Subtropical Fruits*. New York: Hafner Press, 1948.

Prinsky, Roslyn Tamara. "Mangoes in the Caribbean: Production and Postharvest Treatment." Report and recommendations from a study visit, CSC Technical Publication Series No. 203, 1986.

Raafat, Samir. "Remembering the Mango Nuggets." *Egyptian Mail* (www.egy.com/people/94-07-06).

Ramnarain, G., and D. Lakhan. "Mango Improvement in Guyana." *The Farm Journal of Guyana*, 3:1 (April 1999): 32–34.

Reynolds, C. Roy. "The Versatile Mango." *The* (Kingston) *Daily Gleaner* (October 3, 1968): 1, 3.

Sahni, Julie. "Mango Madness." *The* (Hollywood, Florida) *Sun-Tattler* (June 9, 1989): 1, 2C.

Schmitt, Robert C., and Ronn Ronck, eds. *Firsts and Almost Firsts in Hawai'i.* Honolulu: University of Hawai'i Press, 1995.

Senior, Olive. *A–Z of Jamaican Heritage.* Kingston: Heinemann Educational Books (Caribbean) Ltd./The Gleaner Co., Ltd., 1983.

Singh, Lal Behari. *The Mango: Botany, Cultivation and Utilization.* (World Crops Books, N. Polunin, general editor) London: Leonard Hill Ltd./Interscience Publishers, Inc., 1960.

"Story of the Mango." *The* (Kingston) *Cosmopolitan.* (September 1928): 150–1, 156.

Sturrock, David. *Fruits for Southern Florida.* Stuart, Florida: Southeastern Printing Co., Inc., 1959.

"Three-Day Mango Festival Opens in New Delhi." *The* (Bombay*) Financial Express* (http://financialexpress.com/Fe/daily/19990710/flel0005p.).

Thuma, Cindy. "Mangoes Enjoy Exotic Tie to History." *The Hollywood* (Florida) *Sun.* (June 6, 1991): 1B.

Turner, Fred. "The Mango." *New South Wales Agricultural Gazette*, Vol. 1 (1890): 60–62.

Vogelzang, Laurens. "Bush Mango as Alternative to the Chain Saw." *Wisp'r* (Wagenings Universiteitsblad Online), No. 4 (1997): 1. (www.wav.nl/wub/w970401).

Wanitprapha, Wanit, Kevin Nakamoto Yokoyama, Stuart Chia, and C. L. Chia. "Mango." Economic Fact Sheet #16, Department of Agriculture and Resource Economics, College of Tropical Agriculture and Human Resources, University of Hawaii at Manoa, November 1991.

Wester, P. J. "A Contribution to the History of the Mango in Florida." *Mango Studies* (1951): 9–11.

Wolstenholme, B. Nigel, and Anthony W. Whiley. "Ecophysiology of the Mango Tree as a Basis for Preharvest Management." Proceedings from Mango 2000 Marketing Seminar and Production Workshop, Townsville, Australia, 1995.

"Woman Pays Mango's Price with Her Life." *The* (New Delhi) *Hindustan Times* (online edition) (June 30, 1998).

"World market for mango." RAP Market Information Bulletin No. 9, Global Agribusiness Information Network.

Yee, Warren. "The Mango in Hawaii." Cooperative Extension Service, Circular #388, University of Hawaii, June 1981.

Young, T. W., and Julian W. Sauls. "The Mango Industry in Florida." Florida Cooperative Extension Service, Institute of Food and Agricultural Science, Bulletin 189.

Index

NOTE: Information contained in Appendices 1 and 2 has not been indexed.

A

accompaniments
Bes' Kine Mango Salsa, 50
Mangoes Mexicana with Pico Seco, 51
Mexican Mango- Jicama Salsa, 52
Africa, 8
Akbar the Great, 5
Alan Smith Tropical Fruit Trees, 124
amchur, 24
Amroha, 5
Andaman Islands, 8
Anupiya, 5
appetizers
Coconut Shrimp with Mango-Lemon Dip, 34
Mango-Pineapple Rollups, 37
Arampali, 5
Arizona, 9, 11
Athletes' Punch Pops, 82
Augusan del Norte (Philippines), 128
Australia, 9, 11
Austria, 7
Azores, 9

B

B Sting, 66
bacang, 15
Bahamas, 9
Bali, 5
Bangalore (India), 127
Bangladesh, 16
Barbados, 8
Bauna, 15, 16
Bay Street Blast, 78
Bes' Kine Mango Salsa, 50

Binjal, 16
Birdwood Nursery, 123
Blind Hog Groves, 124
Boca Raton, FL, 129
Borneo, 15, 16
Boynton Beach, FL, 124
Bradenton, FL, 126
Brazil, 8, 128
Brazilian pepper, 17
Brevard County (FL), 10,125
Brevard Rare Fruit Council, 125
Brezhnev, Leonid, 6
Brookstone's Wonderland, 124
Broward County (FL), 10
Broward County Rare Fruit and Vegetable Council, 126
Buddha, 5
Buddhism, 5
Buffet, Jimmy, 3
Bulganin, Nicolai, 6
Burma, 8
bush mango, 16

C

California Rare Fruit Growers, Inc., 125
California, 9, 11
Caloosa Rare Fruit Exchange, 126
calorics, 17
Cameroon, 4, 16
carbohydrates, 17
Caribbean, 9
Carter, Jimmy, 6
Cebu City (Philippines), 6, 127
Central America, 9
Chandigarh (India), 128
Cherry-Mangoberry Frozen Fruit Pops, 82

chicken
Chicken Stir-fry with Mangoes and
Asian Corn, 44
Grilled Chicken with Pineapple-
Mango Salsa, 45
Islander Chicken, 47
Chicken Stir-fry with Mangoes and
Asian Corn, 44
China, 6, 8
cholesterol, 17
Chunda, 5
Cisneros, Sandra, 4
Citrus County (FL), 10
Coachella Valley, CA, 11
Coconut Shrimp with Mango-Lemon
Dip, 34
Corcoran, Tom, 4
Costa Rica, 7
CrimeWriters of Queensland, 4
Cryptorhynchus mangiferae, 9
Cuba, 10
Cyprus, 9

D

Daiei (supermarket), 7
Darbhanga, 5
David's Garden Nursery, 124
Davie, FL, 125, 126, 128
de León, Ponce, 10
Deerfield Beach Mango Festival, 128
Deerfield Beach, FL, 128
desserts
Mango Mousse, 57
Mango-Pineapple Drop Cookies, 60
Spiced Stewed Mangoes, 58
Sticky Rice with Mangoes, 56
Summer Fruit Salsa, 59
Upside-Down-Under Cake, 62
Wikiwiki Fresh Fruit Dessert, 63
Dimbulah (Australia), 127
drinks
alcoholic
Bay Street Blast, 78
Frozen Mango Daiquiri, 76
Frozen Mango Margarita, 77

Keys Sunset, 79
Mango Colada, 76
Mangria, 77
Mariposa, 80
Sunspot, 79
nonalcoholic
B Sting, 66
Gardener's Punch, 68
Mango Juice, 69
Mango Milkshake with Cream of
Coconut, 67
Mango Milkshake, 66
Mango-Orange Frost, 70
Miss Mattie's Front Porch Cooler,
71
Traditional Lassi, 72
Tropical Lassi, 72
Whitecap Tropical Freeze, 73
Dussheri Village, 6

E

Eat Mangoes Nude, 4
Edison Keith Mansion, 127
Egypt, 8, 12
Ellman, Lucy, 4
Enomoto, Catherine Kekoa, 98
entrees
Chicken Stir-fry with Mangoes and
Asian Corn, 44
Grilled Chicken with Pineapple-
Mango Salsa, 45
Grilled Pork Chops with Mangoes,
46
Islander Chicken, 47
Last Key Shrimp Kabobs, 48

F

Fairchild Tropical Garden, 123, 126,
128
Fairchild, David, 126
fiber, 17
Florida Department of Agriculture
and Consumer Services, 98
Florida, 9, 28, 98, 124, 125, 126, 127,
128, 129

Food Network, 98
Ford, Henry, 3
Front Street Civic Center, 126
Frozen Mango Daiquiri, 76
Frozen Mango Margarita, 77
Fruit and Spice Park, 126
Fruit Gardener Magazine, The, 125
Ft. Myers, FL, 126

G

Garden of Delights, 125
Gardener's Punch, 68
Gaza Strip, 11
Ghalib, Mirza Asadullah Khan, 3
Ghandi, Indira, 6
Golden Gate Community Center, 128
Gonzalez, Elián, 69
Grand Avenue Mango Salad, 35
Grapeland Nursery, 124
Green Mango Magic, 4
Grilled Chicken with Pineapple-
    Mango Salsa, 45
Grilled Pork Chops with Mangoes, 46
Gugelyk, Ted, 4
Guinea, 9

H

Haas, Robin, 4
Harlee Auditorium, 126
Hart, Benjamin Franklin, 10
Haskelberg Nursery, 125
Hawaii, 9, 10, 24, 28, 125
HEB supermarkets, 7
Herrera, Susana, 4
Hillsborough County (FL), 10
Hilo, HI, 125
Hinduism, 6, 18
Hindustan, 5, 8
Homestead, FL , 126
Honolulu Star-Bulletin, 98
Hornsby, Dale, 4
horse mango, 15
Hossack, Sylvie, 4
House on Mango Street, 4

I

Imamura Nursery, 125
India, 6, 7, 8, 9, 14, 16, 18, 24, 127, 128
Indialantic, FL, 125
Indonesia, 8
International Mango Festival, 123, 126,
    128
International Mango Symposium, 129
International Society for Horticultural
    Science, 129
Irvingia gabonensis, 16
Islander Chicken, 47
Israel, 11, 125

J

J. D. Anderson Nursery, 124
Jamaica, 8
Java, 16
Jivaka, 5

K

Ka'u Mango and Music Festival, 128
Kadison, Joshua, 4
Kasetsart University, 129
Kenya, 9, 24
Key West, 128
Keys Sunset, 79
Kfar Vitkin (Israel), 125
Khmer, 5
Khusran, Amir of, 5
King Mango Strut, 11
King Tissa of Anuradhapura, 5
Kosygin, Alexi, 6
Krishna, Lord, 18
Kruschev, Nikita, 6
Kuini (Kuwini), 15, 16
Kulfi and Kulfi Kones for Kids, 84

L

Laghbakh, 5
Lara Farms Nursery, 124
Las Olas Seafood Salad, 36

137

Last Key Shrimp Kabobs, 48
Last Mango in Paris, 3
Lee County (FL), 126
Louisiana, 9
Luther, Jean M., 4

M

Mahachunda, 5
Mahinda, Prince, 5
Malaysia, 5, 8, 15, 16
Manatee Rare Fruit Council, 126
manga-monjet, 16
Mangifera altissima, 16
Mangifera caesia, 16
Mangifera foetida, 15
Mangifera indica, 8, 15
Mangifera laurina, 16
Mangifera odorata, 15
Mangifera panjang, 15
Mangifera sylvatica, 8
Mangifera verticillata, 15
Mangifera zeylanica, 16
mango
   cultivars
      Alphonso, 6
      Bombay, 124
      Brooks, 14, 30
      Buxton Spice, 124
      Carrie, 124, 125
      Cedar Bay, 30
      Chandrakaran, 13, 27
      Chuchua, 124
      Duncan, 30
      Edgehill, 124
      Edward, 124
      Falan, 30
      Gaylour, 30
      Glenn, 124
      Golek, 30
      Gow, 30
      Haden, 124
      Hong Sa, 30
      Ice Cream, 14
      Ivory, 30
      Jakarta, 124

Julie, 124, 125
Kaimata, 30
Kalmi, 13, 27
Keitt, 11, 13, 124
Kent, 13, 124
Keow, 30
Keow Savoey, 30
Kesar, 14
Lebmue Dam, 30
Lin Ngo Hou, 30
Maha Janka 30
Manila, 124
Mun, 30
Nam Doc Mai, 16, 124
Nang Klang Wan, 16, 30
New Guinea Long, 30
Ngot, 30
Nong Sang, 30
Nuwan Chan, 30
Okrung, 124, 125
Ora, 124
Pim Saen Mun, 30, 124
Rad, 30
Saiphon, 30
Sungi Siput, 30
Tekin, 30
Toledo, 125
Tommy Atkins, 124
Tong Dum, 14, 30
Totapari, 16
Tuong, 30
Valencia Pride, 124
Xoai Tuong, 30
Zill, 13
  dermatitis, 17
  fork, 23
  kernel oil, 24
  marriage, 18, 19
  varieties
    Indian, 13
    Indochinese, 13
    Philippine 13
    wood, 24
Mango Bash, 128
Mango Cats, 3

Mango Colada, 76
Mango Days: A Teenager Facing Eternity Reflects on the Beauty of Life, 4
Mango Elephants in the Sun, 4
Mango Festival, 128
Mango Gang, 4
Mango Granita, 86
Mango Juice, 69
Mango Lady and Other Stories from Hawaii, 4
Mango Leather, 90
Mango Mania, 128
Mango Mela, 127
Mango Milkshake with Cream of Coconut, 67
Mango Milkshake, 66
Mango Mousse, 57
Mango Nut Bread, 91
Mango Opera, The, 4
Mango Utsav, 128
Mango, FL, 10, 128
Mango-Coconut Ice Lollies, 83
mangoes
    freezing, 28, 29
    frozen
        Athletes' Punch Pops, 82
        Cherry-Mangoberry Frozen Fruit Pops, 82
        Kulfi and Kulfi Kones for Kids, 84
        Mango Granita, 86
        Mango-Coconut Ice Lollies, 83
        Thai Ice Pops, 87
    slicing, 26, 27
    storing, 28, 29
    "sucking," 27
Mangoes Mexicana with Pico Seco, 51
MangoMania, 127
Mango-Orange Frost, 70
Mango-Pineapple Drop Cookies, 60
Mango-Pineapple Rollups, 37
Mango-Poppy Seed Vinaigrette Dressing, 93
Man or Mango: A Lament, 4
Mangonia Park, FL, 11

Mangria, 77
Marin, Don Francisco de Paula, 9
Mariposa, 80
Maui, HI, 9
Mauritius, 9
Meek, John, 9
Membangang, 15
Merritt Island, FL, 10
Mexican Mango-Jicama Salsa, 52
Mexico, 9, 128
Miami Herald, 98
Miami, 124, 125, 126
Miami-Dade County (FL), 126
Militello, Mark, 4
Mindanao Mango Congress, 129
minerals, 17
Miss Mattie's Front Porch Cooler, 71
Mounts Botanical Gardens, 127
Murder Under the Mangoes, 4
Mutchilba's Mango Mardi Gras, 127
Myanmar, 8

N

Naples Mango Festival, 128
Naples, FL, 128
Navratilova, Martina, 3
Neeld, W. P., 10
Nehru, Jawaharal, 6
New Delhi, 128
Nokomis, FL, 127
Northwood Hills Mango Festival, 128
nubbins, 14

O

Oahu, HI, 9
Oakland Park, FL, 10
Oba, 3
Old Japanese Mill Camp, 128
Oman, 9
Ono Ono Tropical Bagel Spread, 95

P

Pahala Community Center, 128
Pahala, HI, 128
Pahutan, 16
Pakistan, 6, 9, 128
Palm Bay, FL, 125
Palm Beach Chapter Rare Fruit
    Council Inc., 127
Palm Beach County (FL), 11, 129
Palm Beach Post, 98
Palm Beach, FL, 127
Palmetto, FL, 126
panicles, 13, 14
Pattaya (Thailand), 129
Pavarika, 5
Pelaez Street, 6
peppertree, 15
Perrine, Henry, 10
Persia, 5
Philippine National Mango Congress,
    127
Philippines, 5, 6, 8, 16, 127, 128, 129
Phillippi Creek Park, 127
Pine Island Nursery, 124
Pine Island, FL, 127
Pineapple-Mango Slaw, 38
Pinecrest, FL, 128
poison ivy, 17
Portugal, 8
prayer rituals, 18
Prince Rama, 6
Publix (supermarket), 7
Puerto Rico, 8
Puras, Jose, 125

Q

Queensland (Australia), 11, 127

R

Ramayana, 6
Rawlings, Marjorie Kinnan, 3
Ray's Nursery of Miami, 125
Recipe Archive, 98
Redlands, 126

Reunion, 9
Rhus dermatitis, 17
Rio Grande Valley, 9
Rodriguez, Douglas, 4

S

salads
    Grand Avenue Mango Salad, 35
    Las Olas Seafood Salad, 36
    Pineapple-Mango Slaw 38
    Summer Seafood Salad with
        Sesame-Mango Champagne
        Dressing, 40
    Troppo Fruit Salad, 39
    Yaam, 42
salsas
    Bes' Kine Mango Salsa, 50
    Grilled Chicken with Pineapple-
        Mango Salsa, 45
    Mexican Mango-Jicama Salsa, 52
    Summer Fruit Salsa, 59
Sanskrit, 5, 6
Santa Barbara, CA, 11
Sarasota Fruit and Nut Society, 127
Sarasota, FL, 127
Sark, 4
Schinus molle, 15
Sedano's (supermarket), 7
Seffner, FL, 10
Seventeen Ways to Eat a Mango, 4
Shady Maple Market, 7
Shastri, Lal Bahadur, 6
Shaw, George Bernard, 6
Shimabukuro, Betty, 98
shrimp
    Coconut Shrimp with Mango-
        Lemon Dip, 34
    Last Key Shrimp Kabobs, 48
Smith, Patty, 4
Somalia, 8
South Africa, 12
South America, 9
Spiced Stewed Mangoes, 58
Spies, Black Ties & Mango Pies, 4
Sri Lanka, 5, 16

Star Market, 7
Sticky Rice with Mangoes, 56
Sumatra, 16
Summer Fruit Salsa, 59
Summer Seafood Salad with Sesame-
   Mango Champagne Dressing, 40
Sun World International, 11
Sunspot, 79
Sun-Sentinel, 98
Susser, Allen, 4
Swahili, 5
Switzerland, 7

T

T'sang, Hiuen, 8,
Tahiti, 8
Talkatora Indoor Stadium, 128
Tamil, 7
Terry Park, 126
Texas, 9, 11
Thai Ice Pops, 87
Thailand, 8, 12, 14, 129
Tito, Marshall, 6
Traditional Lassi, 72
Tropica Mango Nursery, 123
Tropical Fruit Festival, 128
Tropical Fruit Growers of South
   Florida, 98
Tropical FruitFest, 129
Tropical Lassi, 72
Tropical Trail Mix, 94
Troppo Fruit Salad, 39
Tse-Tung, Mao, 6
tulsi plant, 18

U

Ukraine, 7
Under the Mango Tree, 4
United States, 9, 12, 16
University of San Carlos, 6
Upanishads, 6
Upside-Down-Under Cake, 62

V

Van Aken, Norman, 4
Vedas, 6
Vietnam, 5, 15
vitamins, 17

W

Warburg, Otto, 11
water mango, 16
Watt, D. G., 10
websites
   www.brevardrarefruit.org, 126
   www.caribbeanseeds.com, 125
   www.fl-ag.com/tropical, 98
   www.foodtv.com, 98
   www.freshmangos.com, 98
   www.freshmangos.com, 98
   www.gopbi.com, 98
   www.herald.com, 98
   www.jdandersen.com, 124
   www.persimmon.co.il, 125
   www.recipes.alastra.com, 98
   www.starbulletin.com, 98
   www.sun-sentinel.com, 98
West Africa, 16
West Indies, 9
West Palm Beach, FL, 127, 128
Westminster, CA, 125
Whitecap Tropical Freeze, 73
Wikiwiki Fresh Fruit Dessert, 63
wild mango, 15
Wild Mango, 3
Winn-Dixie (supermarket), 7

Y

Yaam, 42

Z

Zamboanga City (Philippines), 129
Zill High Performance Plants, 125

141

If you enjoyed reading this book, here are some other Pineapple Press titles you might enjoy as well. To request our complete catalog or to place an order, write to Pineapple Press, P.O. Box 3889, Sarasota, Florida 34230, or call 1-800-PINEAPL (746-3275). Or visit our website at www.pineapplepress.com.

The Essential Catfish Cookbook by Janet Cope and Shannon Harper. Mouth-watering recipes that call for succulent catfish and a variety of easy-to find ingredients. Learn about the private life of the captivating catfish and enjoy this Southern delicacy. ISBN 1-56164-201-0 (pb)

Exotic Foods: A Kitchen & Garden Guide by Marian Van Atta. Grow avocado, mango, carambola, guava, kiwi, pomegranate, and other rare delights in your subtropical backyard. Includes planting and growing instructions as well as over one hundred recipes for enjoying your bountiful crops. ISBN 1-56164-215-0 (pb)

Growing Family Fruit and Nut Trees by Marian Van Atta. What better way to celebrate your family than by growing a tree whose delicious fruit will be a yearly reminder of important events? Learn to choose the right trees and to keep them healthy and bountiful. ISBN 1-56164-001-8 (pb)

Mastering the Art of Florida Seafood by Lonnie T. Lynch. Includes tips on purchasing, preparing, and serving fish and shellfish—with alligators thrown in for good measure. Also includes instructions for artistic food placement, food painting techniques, and more. ISBN 1-56164-176-6 (pb)

The Mostly Mullet Cookbook by George "Grif" Griffin. Mulletheads unite! Includes dozens of mullet main dishes, such as Dixie Fried Mullet, Mullet Italiano, Sweet & Sour Mullet, and the Sea Dog Sandwich, as well as mullet-friendly sides and sauces and other great Southern seafood, including Judy's Mullet Butter and Ybor City Street Vendor's Crab Cakes. ISBN 1-56164-147-2 (pb)

The Sunshine State Cookbook by George S. Fichter. Delicious ways to enjoy the familiar and exotic fruits and vegetables that abound in Florida all year round. Includes seafood cooking tips and delectable recipes such as Rummed Pineapple Flambé and Caribbean Curried Lobster. ISBN 1-56164-214-2 (pb)

Notes

Notes

Notes

Notes

Notes